CLASSIC DESSERTS

Eagle® Brand Sweetened Condensed Milk

BEEKMAN HOUSE

© **1989 Borden, Inc.**

Eagle® is a registered trademark of Borden, Inc.

Recipe development: Borden Kitchens
Annie Watts Cloncs, Director
Charlene Sneed, Senior Home Economist

Photography coordination: Mallard Marketing Associates, Inc.

Microwave Cooking: Microwave ovens vary in wattage and power output; cooking times given for microwave directions in this book may need to be adjusted.

Pictured on the front cover (clockwise from upper right): Creamy Lemon Meringue Pie (*see page 17*), Strawberry Cheese Pie (*see page 27*), Easy Peanut Butter Cookies (*see page 90*) and Cheesecake Topped Brownies (*see page 94*).

Pictured on the back cover (clockwise from upper right): Frozen Peppermint Cheesecake (*see page 159*), Creamy Banana Pudding (*see page 133*), Chocolate Coconut Pecan Torte and Black Forest Torte (*see page 64*).

Library of Congress Catalog Card Number: 00-00000

ISBN: 0-517-67592-7

This edition published by:
Beekman House
Distributed by Crown Publishers, Inc.
225 Park Avenue South
New York, NY 10003

Printed and bound in United States by Arcata Graphics/Hawkins

h g f e d c b

Contents

Eagle® Brand
130 Years of Dessert Making

I t's been called "magic" . . . a can of Eagle® Brand
Sweetened Condensed Milk plus a few select ingredients
and the results are, well, like magic! Rich chocolate candies,
moist cookie bars, picture-perfect lemon pies, light and
luscious cheesecakes, fudgy frostings, caramel flans and
creamy smooth ice cream . . . just a few of the classic desserts
made with Eagle Brand.

y lemon filling made
out cooking! . . See page 17

MAGIC RECIPES

•

*Quicker, easier
surer to succeed*

Did you ever hear of a lemon pie filling —
creamy and lemon-y and smooth—that is
made without cooking? See pages 28 to 31
for this and other truly amazing pie recipes.

A miracle here! Every
lovely candy pictured
at the right is made
without going near a
stove! See pages 32 to 34.

And who said ice cream
making is lots of trou-
ble? Expensive? Better
see pages 15 to 17!

**Try a Tasty
Touch of Magic**

10 Luscious Recipes Made Easy
With the Magic of Eagle® Brand
Sweetened Condensed Milk

BORDEN
EAGLE BRAND
SWEETENED CONDENSED MILK

Around the turn of the century, good cooks everywhere began putting Eagle® Brand Sweetened Condensed Milk to work as a dessert maker. An all-natural precooked blend of fresh whole milk and pure sugar, sweetened condensed milk blends almost magically with other ingredients. Because of this quality, preparation time is minimized. Most desserts made with sweetened condensed milk call for few ingredients, and many require little or no cooking.

The convenience and simplicity of cooking with sweetened condensed milk, as well as the delicious results, have confirmed Eagle Brand's place in history as a classic dessert maker. However, Gail Borden, who invented the product, had another idea in mind.

In the mid-1800s food poisoning and other illnesses related to lack of refrigeration and preservation techniques were common. Borden's concern with these problems led him to the development of sweetened condensed milk, a vacuum-cooked milk product that would not spoil when left unrefrigerated. He was granted a patent in 1856, and began selling his product from a push cart in New York. Later he called the product Eagle Brand after the American eagle, recognized as a symbol of pride and high quality.

The Civil War brought Eagle® Brand Sweetened Condensed Milk the recognition required to make it a household item. The military needed milk that would keep well, and Borden's product filled that need. It was publicly praised for saving many lives during that conflict.

Eagle Brand was also credited with significantly lowering the infant mortality rate throughout North America. Gail Borden's discovery provided a milk that would remain safe and wholesome—at that time, an important contribution to the nourishment of infants and children. Since then, other products have been developed which better meet the need for a healthful and nutritious baby formula.

In 1911 The Borden Company established its own "Welfare Department," the forerunner of today's Borden Kitchens. Then, as now, the department's efforts were focused on providing consumers with new ways to use sweetened condensed milk in preparing foods for their families. The cookbooks and magazine ads produced in the past by the Borden Kitchens continue to provide valuable information and contemporary Eagle Brand recipes and serving ideas for American consumers.

In the early 1900s sweetened condensed milk was used extensively as a creamer and sweetener for coffee, tea and cocoa. Ads of 1918 promised a flavor that makes "an early morning frown give way to an all-day smile of satisfaction."

The creamer-sweetener role has endured over the years, and in some parts of the country today, Eagle Brand always accompanies coffee for special guests in the home. In the Beverage section of this book, look for the delicious punches, shakes and drinks made with the rich creamy goodness of Eagle Brand.

The post World War I era brought prosperity to the country—and refrigeration to most kitchens. Eagle® Brand Sweetened Condensed Milk became increasingly popular as a recipe ingredient, especially for desserts.

Among the company's earliest recipe campaigns was one for homemade ice cream made in the new "automatic" refrigerator. Vanilla, chocolate and

strawberry were the favorite flavors then, as they are today.

The popularity and convenience of Eagle Brand as an ice cream ingredient has not changed. Many delicious recipes for creamy smooth ice creams and frozen desserts are featured in this book.

A 1927 Eagle Brand advertisement promised "glorious" pumpkin pie . . . "the kind about which poets have sung . . . the kind of pumpkin pie that cheats the divorce courts . . . pumpkin pie that has made America great!" Whether in pumpkin, chocolate or Cherry Cheese, Eagle Brand remains a key ingredient in "glorious" pies.

The same is true for all kinds of candies and confections where sweetened condensed milk is the rich creamy base for always-smooth foolproof fudge and chewy macaroons. Coconut Macaroons (spelled "cocoanut" in those days), when made with Eagle Brand, were described as "dainty bits of confection that a French pastry chef might well be proud of."

Recipes made with sweetened condensed milk were as easy to prepare then as they are today. Coconut Macaroons, for example, requires only four ingredients. Early Eagle Brand ice cream recipes called for four or five ingredients—the same as today's ice cream recipes. Magic Lemon Meringue Pie, called Lemon Icebox Pie by homemakers of the 1940s, is made with six ingredients, and cooking is required only to brown the meringue. This recipe favorite is presented here as Creamy Lemon Meringue Pie.

Another quick and easy all-time favorite is our Magic Cookie Bars. You may call these luscious chocolate-y cookies "Hello Dolly Bars" or "7-Layer Bars."

The search for cooking convenience was as strong in the mid-1900s as it is today. Borden cookbooks for Eagle® Brand Sweetened Condensed Milk promised convenience with names such as *New Magic in the Kitchen, Magic! Amazing Shortcuts in Cooking* and *Borden's Eagle Brand Magic Recipes*. Eagle Brand ads, as well as the cookbooks, offered convenient, easy recipes that could be "mixed up even by little girls playing with toy kitchens . . . prepared by homemakers 20 minutes before guests arrived for tea . . . appreciated by efficient women."

In 1931 a Borden Kitchens' promotion offered homemakers $25 for their original recipes. The rules called for "recipes in which Eagle Brand makes cooking quicker, easier, surer."

The response was tremendous! Consumers submitted over 80,000 recipes. Among those accepted as award winners were some whose unusual names evoke great curiosity as to their probable nature . . . "Applelicious," "Caramel Lunchettes," "Magic Surprise," "Cellophane Loaf," "Enoch Sundae" and "Maple Cream Foundation."

Eagle® Brand Sweetened Condensed Milk continued to grow in popularity, gaining promotional assistance from Elsie, the Borden Cow. Elsie made her debut in national consumer magazines in 1938 and starred in Borden's exhibit at the New York World's Fair the following year. She attended press parties, charity events and even a debutante ball.

Eventually Elsie replaced the American eagle as the featured logo on the sweetened condensed milk label. By the 1960s Elsie had become America's best known spokes-cow—a recognized symbol of wholesomeness and quality.

Elsie remains a familiar sight in kitchens today. Good cooks throughout the country continue to create desserts with sweetened condensed milk from the can bearing Elsie's image.

Classic Desserts

Over the years, many recipes using Eagle® Brand Sweetened Condensed Milk have become classics. Some were advertising features. Others were created by consumers. Still others were published in Borden cookbooks, dating back to the early 1900s.

The Borden Kitchens has selected the best of these favorites and developed exciting new recipes to create this cookbook. All the recipes were carefully tested in the Borden Kitchens to assure the consistent quality and good taste you've come to expect from Eagle Brand.

This cookbook salutes Eagle® Brand Sweetened Condensed Milk . . . a product that has always provided consumers a convenient, easy way to create a wide variety of delicious *Classic Desserts*.

Clockwise from right: Fresh Fruit
Cheese Pie, Ambrosia Cheese
Pie and Cherry Cheese Pie
(recipes, page 14)

CHERRY CHEESE PIE

Makes one 9-inch pie

1 (9-inch) graham cracker crumb crust
  or baked pastry shell
1 (8-ounce) package cream cheese,
  softened
1 (14-ounce) can Eagle® Brand
  Sweetened Condensed Milk
  (NOT evaporated milk)
⅓ cup ReaLemon® Lemon Juice from
  Concentrate
1 teaspoon vanilla extract
1 (21-ounce) can cherry pie filling,
  chilled

In large mixer bowl, beat cheese until fluffy. Gradually beat in sweetened condensed milk until smooth. Stir in ReaLemon® brand and vanilla. Pour into prepared crust. Chill 3 hours or until set. Top with desired amount of pie filling before serving. Refrigerate leftovers.

Topping Variations:

Fresh Fruit: Omit cherry pie filling. Arrange well-drained fresh strawberries, banana slices (dipped in ReaLemon® brand and well-drained) and blueberries on top of chilled pie. Just before serving, brush fruit with light corn syrup if desired.

Ambrosia: Omit cherry pie filling. In small saucepan, combine ½ cup peach *or* apricot preserves, ¼ cup flaked coconut, 2 tablespoons orange juice *or* orange-flavored liqueur and 2 teaspoons cornstarch; cook and stir until thickened. Remove from heat. Arrange fresh orange sections over top of pie; top with coconut mixture. Chill.

Blueberry: Omit cherry pie filling. In medium saucepan, combine ¼ cup sugar and 1 tablespoon cornstarch; mix well. Add ½ cup water, 2 tablespoons ReaLemon® brand, then 2 cups fresh or dry-pack frozen blueberries; mix well. Bring to a boil; reduce heat and simmer 3 minutes or until thickened and clear. Cool 10 minutes. Spread over pie. Chill.

Cranberry: Omit cherry pie filling. In medium saucepan, combine ⅓ cup sugar and 1 tablespoon cornstarch. Add ½ cup plus 2 tablespoons cold water and 2 cups fresh or dry-pack frozen cranberries; mix well. Bring to a boil; reduce heat and simmer 10 minutes, stirring constantly. Cool 15 minutes. Spread over pie. Chill.

APPLE CHESS PIE

Makes one 9-inch pie

1 (9-inch) unbaked pastry shell
4 eggs
1 (14-ounce) can Eagle® Brand
  Sweetened Condensed Milk
  (NOT evaporated milk)
1 cup applesauce
½ cup margarine or butter, melted
¼ cup ReaLemon® Lemon Juice from
  Concentrate
2 tablespoons cornmeal

Preheat oven to 425°. Bake pastry shell 8 minutes; remove from oven. Reduce oven temperature to 350°. In large mixer bowl, beat eggs. Add remaining ingredients except pastry shell; mix well. Pour into prepared pastry shell. Bake 40 to 45 minutes or until knife inserted near center comes out clean. Cool. Serve warm or chilled. Refrigerate leftovers.

FUDGY PECAN PIE ▲

Makes one 9-inch pie

1 (9-inch) unbaked pastry shell
1 (4-ounce) package sweet cooking
    chocolate *or* 2 (1-ounce) squares
    unsweetened chocolate
¼ cup margarine or butter
1 (14-ounce) can Eagle® Brand
    Sweetened Condensed Milk
    (NOT evaporated milk)
½ cup hot water
2 eggs, well beaten
1 teaspoon vanilla extract
⅛ teaspoon salt
1¼ cups pecan halves or pieces

Preheat oven to 350°. In medium
saucepan, over low heat, melt chocolate
with margarine. Stir in sweetened
condensed milk, hot water and eggs;
mix well. Remove from heat; stir in
remaining ingredients except pastry
shell. Pour into pastry shell. Bake 40 to
45 minutes or until center is set. Cool
slightly. Serve warm or chilled. Garnish
as desired. Refrigerate leftovers.

CHOCOLATE CUSTARD PIE

Makes one 9-inch pie

1 (9-inch) unbaked pastry shell
2 (1-ounce) squares semi-sweet
    chocolate
1 (14-ounce) can Eagle® Brand
    Sweetened Condensed Milk
    (NOT evaporated milk)
3 eggs, well beaten
1½ cups hot water
2 teaspoons vanilla extract
1 (4-ounce) container frozen non-
    dairy whipped topping, thawed

Preheat oven to 425°. In heavy
saucepan, over low heat, melt chocolate
with sweetened condensed milk.
Remove from heat. Stir in eggs; mix
well. Add hot water and vanilla; mix
well. Pour into pastry shell. Bake 10
minutes. Reduce oven temperature to
300°; continue baking 25 to 30 minutes
or until knife inserted near center comes
out clean. Cool. Chill. Spread whipped
topping over pie. Refrigerate leftovers.

CREAMY LEMON MERINGUE PIE

Makes one 9-inch pie

1 (9-inch) baked pastry shell *or* graham cracker crumb crust
3 eggs*, separated
1 (14-ounce) can Eagle® Brand Sweetened Condensed Milk (NOT evaporated milk)
½ cup ReaLemon® Lemon Juice from Concentrate
Few drops yellow food coloring, optional
¼ teaspoon cream of tartar
⅓ cup sugar

Preheat oven to 350°. In medium bowl, beat egg yolks; stir in sweetened condensed milk, ReaLemon® brand and food coloring if desired. Pour into prepared pastry shell. In small mixer bowl, beat egg whites with cream of tartar until soft peaks form; gradually add sugar, beating until stiff but not dry. Spread meringue on top of pie, sealing carefully to edge of shell. Bake 12 to 15 minutes or until lightly browned. Cool. Chill. Refrigerate leftovers.

Creamy Lemon Pie: Omit egg whites, cream of tartar and sugar. Prepare pie filling as above. Pour into prepared pastry shell. Bake 8 minutes. Cool. Chill. Top with whipped topping. Garnish as desired.

*Use only Grade A clean, uncracked eggs.

FRESH FRUIT DESSERT PIZZA

Makes one 12-inch pizza

1 (14-ounce) can Eagle® Brand Sweetened Condensed Milk (NOT evaporated milk)
½ cup Borden® Sour Cream
¼ cup ReaLemon® Lemon Juice from Concentrate
1 teaspoon vanilla extract
½ cup margarine or butter, softened
¼ cup firmly packed light brown sugar
1 cup unsifted flour
¼ cup quick-cooking oats
¼ cup finely chopped walnuts
Assorted fresh or canned fruit

Preheat oven to 375°. In medium bowl, combine sweetened condensed milk, sour cream, ReaLemon® brand and vanilla; mix well. Chill. In large mixer bowl, beat margarine and sugar until fluffy; add flour, oats and walnuts. Mix well. On lightly greased pizza pan or baking sheet, press dough into 12-inch circle, forming rim around edge. Prick with fork. Bake 10 to 12 minutes or until golden brown. Cool. Spoon filling evenly over crust. Arrange fruit on top. Chill. Refrigerate leftovers.

Tip: Crust and filling can be made in advance and held until ready to assemble. Cover crust and store at room temperature; store filling in refrigerator.

TRADITIONAL PUMPKIN PIE   SOUR CREAM TOPPED PUMPKIN PIE

TRADITIONAL PUMPKIN PIE

Makes one 9-inch pie

1 (9-inch) unbaked pastry shell
1 (16-ounce) can pumpkin (2 cups)
1 (14-ounce) can Eagle® Brand
   Sweetened Condensed Milk
   (NOT evaporated milk)
2 eggs
1 teaspoon ground cinnamon
½ teaspoon ground ginger
½ teaspoon ground nutmeg
½ teaspoon salt

Preheat oven to 425°. In large mixer bowl, combine all ingredients except pastry shell; mix well. Pour into pastry shell. Bake 15 minutes. Reduce oven temperature to 350°; continue baking 35 to 40 minutes or until knife inserted 1 inch from edge comes out clean. Cool. Garnish as desired. Refrigerate leftovers.

Sour Cream Topping: In medium bowl, combine 1½ cups Borden® Sour Cream, 2 tablespoons sugar and 1 teaspoon vanilla extract. After 30 minutes of baking, spread evenly over top of pie; bake 10 minutes longer. Garnish as desired.

Streusel Topping: In medium bowl, combine ½ cup firmly packed light brown sugar and ½ cup unsifted flour; cut in ¼ cup cold margarine or butter until crumbly. Stir in ¼ cup chopped nuts. After 30 minutes of baking, sprinkle on top of pie; bake 10 minutes longer.

18   Pies

STREUSEL TOPPED PUMPKIN PIE

SPIRITED EGG NOG CUSTARD PIE

Makes one 9-inch pie

1 (9-inch) unbaked pastry shell
1 (14-ounce) can Eagle® Brand Sweetened Condensed Milk (NOT evaporated milk)
1⅓ cups warm water
2 tablespoons light rum
1 tablespoon brandy
1 teaspoon vanilla extract
½ teaspoon ground nutmeg
3 eggs, well beaten

Preheat oven to 425°. Bake pastry shell 8 minutes; remove from oven. In large bowl, combine all ingredients except eggs and pastry shell; mix well. Stir in eggs. Pour into pastry shell. Bake 10 minutes. Reduce oven temperature to 325°; continue baking 25 to 30 minutes or until knife inserted near center comes out clean. Cool. Chill if desired. Refrigerate leftovers.

CREAMY MOCK CHEESE PIE

Makes one 9-inch pie

1 (9-inch) graham cracker crumb crust
1 (16-ounce) container Borden® Sour Cream
1 (14-ounce) can Eagle® Brand Sweetened Condensed Milk (NOT evaporated milk)
3 tablespoons presweetened lemonade flavor drink mix
Peach preserves, optional

Preheat oven to 350°. In medium bowl, combine sour cream, sweetened condensed milk and drink mix; mix well. Pour into prepared crust. Bake 25 to 30 minutes. Cool. Chill at least 2 hours. Garnish with preserves if desired. Refrigerate leftovers.

Tip: Other fruit preserves can be substituted for peach preserves.

MILLION DOLLAR PIES

Makes 2 pies

1 (3½-ounce) can flaked coconut
   (1⅓ cups)
1 (14-ounce) can Eagle® Brand
   Sweetened Condensed Milk
   (NOT evaporated milk)
1 (20-ounce) can juice-pack crushed
   pineapple *or* 1 (29-ounce) can
   fruit cocktail, *well drained*
1 cup coarsely chopped pecans
¼ cup ReaLemon® Lemon Juice from
   Concentrate
1 (8-ounce) container frozen non-
   dairy whipped topping, thawed
2 (6-ounce) packaged graham cracker
   crumb pie crusts

Toast ⅓ *cup* coconut; set aside. In large
bowl, combine sweetened condensed
milk, pineapple, remaining *1 cup*
coconut, pecans and ReaLemon® brand;
mix well. Fold in whipped topping.
Pour into crusts. Garnish with toasted
coconut. Chill 3 hours or until set.
Refrigerate leftovers.

Million Dollar Dessert Squares: In
medium bowl, combine ½ cup
margarine or butter, melted, 1¼ cups
graham cracker crumbs and ¼ cup
sugar; mix well. Press firmly on bottom
of 13×9-inch baking dish. Chill. Prepare
filling as above; spread evenly over
crust. Top with toasted coconut. Chill as
above.

APPLE CUSTARD TART

Makes one 9- or 10-inch pie

1 (9- or 10-inch) unbaked pastry shell
1½ cups Borden® Sour Cream
1 (14-ounce) can Eagle® Brand
   Sweetened Condensed Milk
   (NOT evaporated milk)
¼ cup frozen apple juice concentrate,
   thawed
1 egg
1½ teaspoons vanilla extract
¼ teaspoon ground cinnamon
2 medium all-purpose apples, cored,
   pared and thinly sliced (about
   2 cups)
1 tablespoon margarine or butter
   Apple Cinnamon Glaze

Preheat oven to 375°. Bake pastry shell
15 minutes. Meanwhile, in small mixer
bowl, beat sour cream, sweetened
condensed milk, juice concentrate, egg,
vanilla and cinnamon until smooth.
Pour into prepared pastry shell; bake 30
minutes or until set. Cool. In large
skillet, cook apples in margarine until
tender-crisp. Arrange on top of pie;
drizzle with Apple Cinnamon Glaze.
Refrigerate leftovers.

Apple Cinnamon Glaze: In small
saucepan, combine ¼ cup frozen apple
juice concentrate, thawed, 1 teaspoon
cornstarch and ¼ teaspoon ground
cinnamon; mix well. Over low heat,
cook and stir until thickened. (Makes
about ¼ cup)

BANANA SPLIT DESSERT PIZZA

Makes one 12-inch pizza

1 (14-ounce) can Eagle® Brand
   Sweetened Condensed Milk
   (NOT evaporated milk)
½ cup Borden® Sour Cream
6 tablespoons ReaLemon® Lemon
   Juice from Concentrate
1 teaspoon vanilla extract
½ cup plus 1 tablespoon margarine or
   butter, softened
¼ cup firmly packed brown sugar
1 cup unsifted flour
¼ cup quick-cooking oats
¼ cup finely chopped nuts
3 medium bananas, sliced
1 (8-ounce) can sliced pineapple,
   drained and cut in half
   Maraschino cherries and nuts
1 (1-ounce) square semi-sweet
   chocolate

Preheat oven to 375°. In medium bowl, combine sweetened condensed milk, sour cream, ¼ cup ReaLemon® brand and vanilla; mix well. Chill. In large mixer bowl, beat ½ cup margarine and sugar until fluffy; add flour, oats and nuts. Mix well. On lightly greased pizza pan or baking sheet, press dough into 12-inch circle, forming rim around edge. Prick with fork. Bake 10 to 12 minutes or until golden brown. Cool. Arrange 2 bananas on cooled crust. Spoon filling evenly over bananas. Dip remaining banana slices in remaining 2 *tablespoons* ReaLemon® brand; arrange on top along with pineapple, cherries and additional nuts. In small saucepan, over low heat, melt chocolate with remaining 1 *tablespoon* margarine; drizzle over pie. Chill. Refrigerate leftovers.

Tip: Crust and filling can be made in advance and held until ready to assemble. Cover crust and store at room temperature; store filling in refrigerator.

CRANBERRY CRUMB PIE

Makes one 9-inch pie

1 (9-inch) unbaked pastry shell
1 (8-ounce) package cream cheese,
    softened
1 (14-ounce) can Eagle® Brand
    Sweetened Condensed Milk
    (NOT evaporated milk)
¼ cup ReaLemon® Lemon Juice from
    Concentrate
3 tablespoons light brown sugar
2 tablespoons cornstarch
1 (16-ounce) can whole berry
    cranberry sauce
¼ cup cold margarine or butter
⅓ cup unsifted flour
¾ cup chopped walnuts

Preheat oven to 425°. Bake pastry shell 8 minutes; remove from oven. Reduce oven temperature to 375°. In large mixer bowl, beat cheese until fluffy. Gradually beat in sweetened condensed milk until smooth. Stir in ReaLemon® brand. Pour into pastry shell. In small bowl, combine 1 *tablespoon* sugar and cornstarch; mix well. Stir in cranberry sauce. Spoon evenly over cheese mixture. In medium bowl, cut margarine into flour and remaining 2 *tablespoons* sugar until crumbly. Stir in nuts. Sprinkle evenly over cranberry mixture. Bake 45 to 50 minutes or until bubbly and golden. Cool. Serve at room temperature or chill. Refrigerate leftovers.

Preheat oven to 350°. In large heavy saucepan, over low heat, melt chocolate with margarine. Stir in sweetened condensed milk, water and eggs; *mix well*. Remove from heat; stir in remaining ingredients except pastry shell. Pour into pastry shell. Bake 35 to 40 minutes or until center is set. Cool. Serve warm or chilled. Garnish as desired. Refrigerate leftovers.

MICROWAVE CARAMEL NUT CREAM PIE

Makes 1 pie

1 (14-ounce) can Eagle® Brand
    Sweetened Condensed Milk
    (NOT evaporated milk)
1 cup chopped nuts
2 tablespoons Borden® Milk
½ teaspoon ground cinnamon
1 cup (½ pint) Borden® Whipping
    Cream, whipped
1 (6-ounce) packaged graham cracker
    crumb pie crust

Pour sweetened condensed milk into 2-quart glass measure. Cook on 50% power (medium) 4 minutes, stirring briskly every 2 minutes until smooth. Cook on 30% power (medium-low) 12 to 18 minutes or until caramel-colored, stirring briskly every 2 minutes until smooth. Stir nuts, milk and cinnamon into *warm* caramelized sweetened condensed milk; cool. Chill. Fold in whipped cream. Pour into crust. Chill 3 hours or until set. Garnish as desired. Refrigerate leftovers.

CAUTION: NEVER HEAT UNOPENED CAN.

CHOCO-CHERRY MACAROON PIE

Makes one 9-inch pie

1 (9-inch) unbaked pastry shell
2 (1-ounce) squares unsweetened
    chocolate
¼ cup margarine or butter
1 (14-ounce) can Eagle® Brand
    Sweetened Condensed Milk
    (NOT evaporated milk)
¾ cup hot water
2 eggs, well beaten
1 teaspoon vanilla extract
⅛ teaspoon salt
1 (3½-ounce) can flaked coconut
    (1⅓ cups)
½ cup red candied cherries, chopped

MINI FRUIT CHEESE TARTS

Makes 24 tarts

24 (2- or 3-inch) prepared tart-size
   crusts
1 (8-ounce) package cream cheese,
   softened
1 (14-ounce) can Eagle® Brand
   Sweetened Condensed Milk
   (NOT evaporated milk)
⅓ cup ReaLemon® Lemon Juice from
   Concentrate
1 teaspoon vanilla extract
   Assorted fruit (strawberries,
   blueberries, bananas, raspberries,
   orange segments, cherries,
   kiwifruit, grapes or pineapple
¼ cup apple jelly, melted

In large mixer bowl, beat cheese until
fluffy. Gradually beat in sweetened
condensed milk until smooth. Stir in
ReaLemon® brand and vanilla. Spoon
equal portions into crusts. Top with
fruit; brush with jelly. Chill 2 hours or
until set. Refrigerate leftovers.

BANANA MANDARIN CHEESE PIE

Makes one 9-inch pie

1 (9-inch) graham cracker crumb crust
1 (8-ounce) package cream cheese,
   softened
1 (14-ounce) can Eagle® Brand
   Sweetened Condensed Milk
   (NOT evaporated milk)
⅓ cup ReaLemon® Lemon Juice from
   Concentrate
1 teaspoon vanilla extract
3 medium bananas
   Additional ReaLemon® brand
1 (11-ounce) can mandarin orange
   segments, well drained

In large mixer bowl, beat cheese until fluffy. Gradually beat in sweetened condensed milk until smooth. Stir in ⅓ *cup* ReaLemon® brand and vanilla. Slice *2 bananas*; dip in ReaLemon® brand. Drain and line crust with bananas and about *two-thirds* of the orange segments. Pour filling over fruit. Chill 3 hours or until set. Before serving, slice remaining *1 banana*; dip in ReaLemon® brand and drain. Arrange remaining banana slices and orange segments on top of pie. Refrigerate leftovers.

LEMON ICEBOX PIE

Makes one 9-inch pie

1½ cups vanilla wafer crumbs (about 45 wafers)
¼ cup margarine or butter, melted
1 envelope unflavored gelatine
1½ cups water
1 (14-ounce) can Eagle® Brand Sweetened Condensed Milk (NOT evaporated milk)
1 (3-ounce) package *or* 6 tablespoons presweetened lemonade flavor drink mix

Combine crumbs and margarine. Press firmly on bottom and up side to rim of 9-inch pie plate; chill. In small saucepan, sprinkle gelatine over ¼ *cup* water; let stand 1 minute. Over low heat, stir until dissolved. In medium bowl, combine sweetened condensed milk, remaining 1¼ *cups* water and drink mix; mix well. Stir in gelatine mixture. Pour into prepared crust. Chill 3 hours or until set. Garnish as desired. Refrigerate leftovers.

CREAMY NESSELRODE PIE

Makes one 9-inch pie

Chocolate Coconut Crust
1 envelope unflavored gelatine
¼ cup orange juice
1 (14-ounce) can Eagle® Brand Sweetened Condensed Milk (NOT evaporated milk)
¼ cup Borden® Sour Cream
2 tablespoons light rum
½ cup chopped mixed candied fruit
½ cup chopped nuts
¼ cup raisins
1 cup (½ pint) Borden® Whipping Cream, whipped

Prepare Chocolate Coconut Crust. In small saucepan, sprinkle gelatine over orange juice; let stand 1 minute. Over low heat, stir until gelatine dissolves. In large bowl, combine sweetened condensed milk, sour cream, gelatine mixture and rum. Chill until mixture mounds slightly when dropped from spoon, about 30 minutes. Fold in fruit, nuts, raisins and whipped cream. Pour into prepared crust. Chill 4 hours or until set. Garnish as desired. Refrigerate leftovers.

Chocolate Coconut Crust: In large saucepan, over low heat, melt 2 tablespoons margarine or butter with 1 (1-ounce) square unsweetened chocolate. Add 1 (7-ounce) package (2⅔ cups) flaked coconut. Mix well. Press firmly on bottom and up side to rim of 9-inch pie plate. Chill.

STRAWBERRY CHEESE PIE

Makes one 9-inch pie

1 (9-inch) baked pastry shell *or*
   graham cracker crumb crust
1 (8-ounce) package cream cheese,
   softened
1 (14-ounce) can Eagle® Brand
   Sweetened Condensed Milk
   (NOT evaporated milk)
⅓ cup ReaLemon® Lemon Juice from
   Concentrate
1 teaspoon vanilla extract
1 quart fresh strawberries, cleaned
   and hulled
1 (16-ounce) package prepared
   strawberry glaze, chilled

In large mixer bowl, beat cheese until
fluffy. Gradually beat in sweetened
condensed milk until smooth. Stir in
ReaLemon® brand and vanilla. Pour into
prepared crust. Chill 3 hours or until
set. Top with strawberries and desired
amount of glaze. Refrigerate leftovers.

FLUFFY YOGURT FRUIT PIE

Makes one 9-inch pie

1 (9-inch) graham cracker crumb crust
1 (8-ounce) package cream cheese,
   softened
1 (14-ounce) can Eagle® Brand
   Sweetened Condensed Milk
   (NOT evaporated milk)
1 (8-ounce) container Borden® Lite-
   line® Strawberry or other Fruit
   Yogurt
2 tablespoons ReaLemon® Lemon
   Juice from Concentrate
2 to 3 drops red or other food
   coloring, optional
1 (8-ounce) container frozen non-
   dairy whipped topping, thawed
Strawberries or other fresh fruit

In large mixer bowl, beat cheese until
fluffy. Gradually beat in sweetened
condensed milk until smooth. Stir in
yogurt, ReaLemon® brand and food
coloring if desired. Fold in whipped
topping. Pour into prepared crust.
Garnish with strawberries. Chill 4 hours
or until set. Refrigerate leftovers.

EASY LEMON PUDDING PIE

Makes one 9-inch pie

Coconut Crust
1 (4-serving size) package *instant*
   lemon flavor pudding mix
1 cup cold water
1 (8-ounce) package cream cheese,
   softened
1 (14-ounce) can Eagle® Brand
   Sweetened Condensed Milk
   (NOT evaporated milk)
1 teaspoon grated lemon rind
1 (4-ounce) container frozen non-
   dairy whipped topping, thawed

Prepare Coconut Crust. In small mixer
bowl, on low speed, beat pudding mix
and water until smooth. In large mixer
bowl, beat cheese until fluffy. Gradually
beat in sweetened condensed milk until
smooth. Stir in pudding mixture and
rind. Fold in whipped topping. Pour
into prepared crust. Chill 3 hours or
until set. Garnish as desired. Refrigerate
leftovers.

Coconut Crust: Preheat oven to 325°.
In medium bowl, combine 1 (7-ounce)
package flaked coconut (2⅔ cups) and
3 tablespoons margarine or butter,
melted. Press firmly on bottom and up
side to rim of 9-inch pie plate. Bake 20
minutes or until golden brown. Cool.

TROPICAL LIME PIE ▲

Makes one 9-inch pie

2½ cups flaked coconut, toasted
⅓ cup margarine or butter, melted
1 (8-ounce) package cream cheese, softened
1 (14-ounce) can Eagle® Brand Sweetened Condensed Milk (NOT evaporated milk)
⅓ cup ReaLime® Lime Juice from Concentrate
Few drops green food coloring, optional
1 (4-ounce) container frozen non-dairy whipped topping, thawed

Combine coconut and margarine; press firmly on bottom and up side to rim of 9-inch pie plate. Chill. Meanwhile, in large mixer bowl, beat cheese until fluffy. Gradually beat in sweetened condensed milk, then ReaLime® brand and food coloring if desired until smooth. Fold in whipped topping. Pour into prepared crust. Chill 3 hours or until set. Garnish as desired. Refrigerate leftovers.

IMPOSSIBLE PIE

Makes one 10-inch pie

1 (14-ounce) can Eagle® Brand Sweetened Condensed Milk (NOT evaporated milk)
1½ cups water
½ cup biscuit baking mix
3 eggs
¼ cup margarine or butter, softened
1½ teaspoons vanilla extract
1 cup flaked coconut

Preheat oven to 350°. In blender container, combine all ingredients except coconut. Blend on low speed 3 minutes. Pour mixture into buttered 10-inch pie plate; let stand 5 minutes. Sprinkle coconut over top. Carefully place in oven; bake 35 to 40 minutes or until knife inserted near edge comes out clean. Cool slightly; serve warm or cool. Refrigerate leftovers.

Tip: Pie can be baked in buttered 9-inch pie plate but it will be extremely full.

Impossible Lemon Pie: Add 3 tablespoons ReaLemon® Lemon Juice from Concentrate and 1 tablespoon grated lemon rind to ingredients in blender.

FLUFFY ORANGE PIE

Makes one 9-inch pie

2 cups vanilla wafer crumbs (about 50 wafers)
⅓ cup margarine or butter, melted
1 (8-ounce) package cream cheese, softened
1 (14-ounce) can Eagle® Brand Sweetened Condensed Milk (NOT evaporated milk)
1 (6-ounce) can frozen orange juice concentrate, thawed
1 cup (½ pint) Borden® Whipping Cream, whipped

Combine crumbs and margarine; press firmly on bottom and up side to rim of 9-inch pie plate. Chill. Meanwhile, in large mixer bowl, beat cheese until fluffy. Gradually beat in sweetened condensed milk until smooth. Stir in juice concentrate. Fold in whipped cream. Pour into crust. Chill 2 hours or until set. Garnish as desired. Refrigerate leftovers.

AVOCADO CHEESE PIE

Makes one 9-inch pie

1 (9-inch) graham cracker crumb crust
1 (8-ounce) package cream cheese, softened
1 (14-ounce) can Eagle® Brand Sweetened Condensed Milk (NOT evaporated milk)
1 ripe medium avocado, mashed or pureed (about ½ cup)
½ cup ReaLime® Lime Juice from Concentrate
¼ teaspoon salt
Few drops green food coloring, optional
Whipped cream, optional

In large mixer bowl, beat cheese until fluffy. Gradually beat in sweetened condensed milk, then avocado until smooth. Stir in ReaLime® brand, salt and food coloring if desired. Pour into prepared crust. Chill 4 hours or until set. Garnish with whipped cream if desired. Refrigerate leftovers.

FLUFFY ORANGE PIE

CREATE-A-CRUST APPLE PIE

Makes one 10-inch pie

2 medium all-purpose apples, pared and sliced (about 2 cups)
1 tablespoon ReaLemon® Lemon Juice from Concentrate
½ cup plus 2 tablespoons biscuit baking mix
1 (14-ounce) can Eagle® Brand Sweetened Condensed Milk (NOT evaporated milk)
1½ cups water
3 eggs
¼ cup margarine or butter, softened
1½ teaspoons vanilla extract
½ teaspoon ground cinnamon
½ teaspoon ground nutmeg

Preheat oven to 350°. In medium bowl, toss apples with ReaLemon® brand, then *2 tablespoons* biscuit mix. Arrange on bottom of buttered 10-inch pie plate. In blender container, combine remaining ingredients. Blend on low speed 3 minutes. Let stand 5 minutes. Pour evenly over apples. Bake 35 to 40 minutes or until golden brown around edge. Cool slightly; serve warm or chilled with vanilla ice cream. Refrigerate leftovers.

SWEET POTATO PECAN PIE

Makes one 9-inch pie

1 (9-inch) unbaked pastry shell
1 pound (2 medium) yams or sweet potatoes, cooked and peeled
¼ cup margarine or butter
1 (14-ounce) can Eagle® Brand Sweetened Condensed Milk (NOT evaporated milk)
1 teaspoon grated orange rind
1 teaspoon vanilla extract
1 teaspoon ground cinnamon
½ teaspoon ground nutmeg
¼ teaspoon salt
2 eggs
Pecan Topping

Preheat oven to 350°. In large mixer bowl, beat hot yams with margarine until smooth. Add remaining ingredients except pastry shell and Pecan Topping; mix well. Pour into pastry shell. Bake 30 minutes. Remove from oven; spoon Pecan Topping evenly over top. Return to oven; bake 20 to 25 minutes or until golden brown. Cool. Serve warm or chilled. Refrigerate leftovers.

Pecan Topping: In small mixer bowl, combine 1 egg, 3 tablespoons dark corn syrup, 3 tablespoons firmly packed light brown sugar, 1 tablespoon margarine, melted, and ½ teaspoon maple flavoring; mix well. Stir in 1 cup chopped pecans.

COCONUT CUSTARD PIE

Makes one 9-inch pie

- 1 (9-inch) unbaked pastry shell
- 1 cup flaked coconut
- 3 eggs
- 1 (14-ounce) can Eagle® Brand Sweetened Condensed Milk (NOT evaporated milk)
- 1¼ cups hot water
- 1 teaspoon vanilla extract
- ¼ teaspoon salt
- ⅛ teaspoon ground nutmeg

Preheat oven to 425°. Toast *½ cup* coconut; set aside. Bake pastry shell 8 minutes; cool slightly. Meanwhile, in medium bowl, beat eggs. Add sweetened condensed milk, water, vanilla, salt and nutmeg; mix well. Stir in remaining *½ cup* coconut. Pour into pastry shell. Sprinkle with toasted coconut. Bake 10 minutes. Reduce oven temperature to 350°; continue baking 25 to 30 minutes or until knife inserted near center comes out clean. Cool. Chill if desired. Refrigerate leftovers.

Custard Pie: Omit coconut. Proceed as above.

CHOCOLATE ALMOND PIE

Makes one 9-inch pie

- 1 (9-inch) unbaked pastry shell
- 2 (1-ounce) squares unsweetened chocolate
- ¼ cup margarine or butter
- 1 (14-ounce) can Eagle® Brand Sweetened Condensed Milk (NOT evaporated milk)
- ⅓ cup hot water
- 2 eggs, well beaten
- ¼ to ⅓ cup amaretto liqueur
- ⅛ teaspoon salt
- 1 cup slivered almonds, toasted and chopped

Preheat oven to 350°. In medium saucepan, over low heat, melt chocolate with margarine. Stir in sweetened condensed milk, hot water and eggs; *mix well.* Remove from heat; stir in remaining ingredients except pastry shell. Pour into pastry shell. Bake 40 to 45 minutes or until center is set. Cool. Chill 3 hours. Garnish as desired. Refrigerate leftovers.

COCONUT CUSTARD PIE

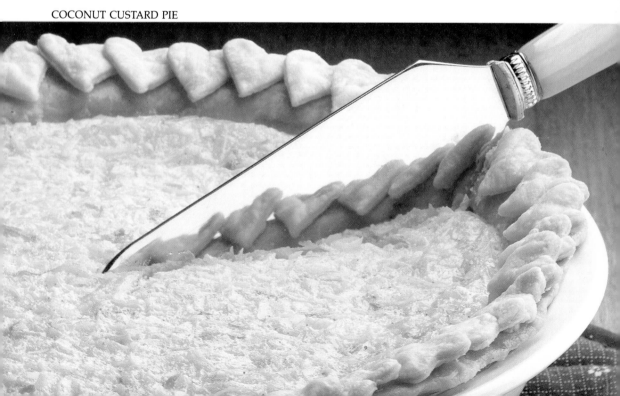

DEEP DISH PUMPKIN PIE

Makes 8 to 10 servings

1¾ cups unsifted flour
⅓ cup firmly packed brown sugar
⅓ cup granulated sugar
1 cup cold margarine or butter, cut
    into small pieces
1 cup chopped nuts
1 (16-ounce) can pumpkin (2 cups)
1 (14-ounce) can Eagle® Brand
    Sweetened Condensed Milk
    (NOT evaporated milk)
2 eggs
1 teaspoon ground cinnamon
½ teaspoon allspice
½ teaspoon salt

Preheat oven to 350°. In medium bowl, combine flour and sugars; cut in margarine until crumbly. Stir in nuts. Reserving 1 cup crumb mixture, press remainder firmly on bottom and halfway up sides of 12×7-inch baking dish. In large mixer bowl, combine remaining ingredients except reserved crumb mixture; mix well. Pour into prepared dish. Top with crumb mixture. Bake 55 minutes or until golden. Cool. Garnish as desired. Refrigerate leftovers.

DEEP DISH PUMPKIN PIE (LEFT), CHOCOLATE AMARETTO PIE (RIGHT)

CHOCOLATE CHIFFON PIE

Makes 1 pie

2 (1-ounce) squares unsweetened
    chocolate
1 (14-ounce) can Eagle® Brand
    Sweetened Condensed Milk
    (NOT evaporated milk)
1 envelope unflavored gelatine
⅓ cup water
½ teaspoon vanilla extract
1 cup (½ pint) Borden® Whipping
    Cream, whipped
1 (6-ounce) packaged chocolate or
    graham cracker crumb pie crust
Additional whipped cream

In heavy saucepan, over low heat, melt chocolate with sweetened condensed milk. Remove from heat. Meanwhile, in small saucepan, sprinkle gelatine over water; let stand 1 minute. Over low heat, stir until gelatine dissolves. Stir into chocolate mixture. Add vanilla. Cool to room temperature. Fold in whipped cream. Pour into crust. Chill 3 hours or until set. Garnish with additional whipped cream. Refrigerate leftovers.

CHOCOLATE AMARETTO PIE

Makes one 9-inch pie

1 (9-inch) unbaked pastry shell
1 (3-ounce) package cream cheese, softened
2 (1-ounce) squares unsweetened chocolate, melted
⅛ teaspoon salt
1 (14-ounce) can Eagle® Brand Sweetened Condensed Milk (NOT evaporated milk)
2 eggs
¼ to ⅓ cup amaretto liqueur
1 cup chopped or sliced almonds, toasted if desired

Preheat oven to 350°. In large mixer bowl, beat cheese, chocolate and salt until well blended. Gradually beat in sweetened condensed milk until smooth. Add eggs; mix well. Stir in liqueur and almonds. Pour into pastry shell. Bake 30 to 35 minutes or until center is set. Cool. Serve warm or chilled. Garnish as desired. Refrigerate leftovers.

GLAZED APPLE CREAM TART

Makes one 9-inch tart

- ½ cup plus 2 tablespoons margarine or butter, softened
- ¼ cup firmly packed light brown sugar
- 1 cup unsifted flour
- ¼ cup quick-cooking oats
- ¼ cup finely chopped walnuts
- 1 (14-ounce) can Eagle® Brand Sweetened Condensed Milk (NOT evaporated milk)
- 1 (16-ounce) container Borden® Sour Cream
- ½ cup frozen apple juice concentrate, thawed
- 2 eggs, beaten
- 1 teaspoon vanilla extract
- 2 medium all-purpose apples, pared and thinly sliced (about 2 cups)
- ½ cup apricot preserves
- 5 teaspoons water
- 1 teaspoon cornstarch

Preheat oven to 350°. In small mixer bowl, beat ½ *cup* margarine and sugar until fluffy. Stir in flour, oats and nuts; press firmly on bottom and halfway up side of lightly greased 9-inch springform pan. Bake 15 to 20 minutes or until golden. Meanwhile, in medium bowl, combine sweetened condensed milk and sour cream; add juice concentrate, eggs and vanilla. Mix well. Pour into prepared crust. Bake 30 to 35 minutes or until center is set. Cool. In medium saucepan, melt remaining *2 tablespoons* margarine. Add apples; cook and stir until tender. Arrange on top of tart. In small saucepan, combine preserves, water and cornstarch; cook and stir until slightly thickened. Spoon over apples. Chill. Refrigerate leftovers.

FLUFFY GRASSHOPPER PIE

Makes one 9-inch pie

2 cups finely crushed creme-filled
　　chocolate sandwich cookies
　　(about 20 cookies)
¼ cup margarine or butter, melted
1 (8-ounce) package cream cheese,
　　softened
1 (14-ounce) can Eagle® Brand
　　Sweetened Condensed Milk
　　(NOT evaporated milk)
3 tablespoons ReaLemon® Lemon
　　Juice from Concentrate
¼ cup green creme de menthe
¼ cup white creme de cacao
1 (4-ounce) container frozen non-
　　dairy whipped topping, thawed

Combine crumbs and margarine; press firmly on bottom and up side to rim of buttered 9-inch pie plate. Chill. Meanwhile, in large mixer bowl, beat cheese until fluffy. Gradually beat in sweetened condensed milk until smooth. Stir in ReaLemon® brand and liqueurs. Fold in whipped topping. Chill 20 minutes; pour into crust. Chill or freeze 4 hours or until set. Garnish as desired. Refrigerate or freeze leftovers.

STREUSEL-TOPPED APPLE CUSTARD PIE

Makes one 9-inch pie

1 (9-inch) unbaked pastry shell
4 medium all-purpose apples, pared and sliced (about 4 cups)
2 eggs
1 (14-ounce) can Eagle® Brand Sweetened Condensed Milk (NOT evaporated milk)
¼ cup margarine or butter, melted
½ teaspoon ground cinnamon
Dash ground nutmeg
½ cup firmly packed light brown sugar
½ cup unsifted flour
¼ cup cold margarine or butter
¼ cup chopped nuts

Place rack in lower third of oven; preheat oven to 425°. Arrange apples in pastry shell. In medium bowl, beat eggs. Add sweetened condensed milk, melted margarine, cinnamon and nutmeg; mix well. Pour over apples. In medium bowl, combine sugar and flour; cut in cold margarine until crumbly. Stir in nuts. Sprinkle over pie. Bake 10 minutes. Reduce oven temperature to 375°; continue baking 35 to 40 minutes or until golden brown. Cool. Refrigerate leftovers.

CANDY APPLE CHEESE PIE

Makes one 9-inch pie

1 (9-inch) baked pastry shell
1 (8-ounce) package cream cheese, softened
1 (14-ounce) can Eagle® Brand Sweetened Condensed Milk (NOT evaporated milk)
⅓ cup ReaLemon® Lemon Juice from Concentrate
1 teaspoon vanilla extract
1 (20-ounce) can sliced apples, *well drained* on paper towels
¼ cup red cinnamon candies
6 tablespoons water
2 teaspoons cornstarch

In large mixer bowl, beat cheese until fluffy. Gradually beat in sweetened condensed milk until smooth. Stir in ReaLemon® brand and vanilla. Pour into prepared pastry shell. Arrange apple slices over top of pie. In small saucepan, over *low* heat, dissolve cinnamon candies in *¼ cup* water. Stir together remaining *2 tablespoons* water and cornstarch; add to cinnamon mixture. Cook and stir until mixture thickens and boils. Remove from heat; cool slightly. Spoon over apples. Chill 3 hours or until set. Refrigerate leftovers.

STREUSEL-TOPPED APPLE CUSTARD PIE (TOP), CANDY APPLE CHEESE PIE (BOTTOM)

PINK LEMONADE PIE ▲

Makes one 9-inch pie

1 (9-inch) baked pastry shell
1 (8-ounce) package cream cheese,
    softened
1 (14-ounce) can Eagle® Brand
    Sweetened Condensed Milk
    (NOT evaporated milk)
1 (6-ounce) can frozen pink lemonade
    concentrate, thawed
    Few drops red food coloring,
    optional
1 (4-ounce) container frozen non-
    dairy whipped topping, thawed
½ cup pink tinted coconut*

In large mixer bowl, beat cheese until
fluffy; gradually beat in sweetened
condensed milk, then lemonade
concentrate and food coloring if desired.
Fold in whipped topping. Pour into
prepared pastry shell. Chill 4 hours or
until set. Garnish with coconut.
Refrigerate leftovers.

To tint coconut: Combine ½ cup flaked
coconut, ½ teaspoon water and 2 drops
red food coloring in small plastic bag or
bowl. Shake or mix well.

ALMOND PUMPKIN PIE

Makes one 9-inch pie

1 (9-inch) unbaked pastry shell
1 (16-ounce) can pumpkin (2 cups)
1 (14-ounce) can Eagle® Brand
    Sweetened Condensed Milk
    (NOT evaporated milk)
2 eggs
½ teaspoon almond extract
½ teaspoon ground cinnamon
1 (6-ounce) package almond brickle
    chips

Preheat oven to 425°. In large mixer
bowl, combine all ingredients except
pastry shell and brickle chips; mix well.
Stir in ½ cup brickle chips. Pour into
pastry shell. Top with remaining brickle
chips. Bake 15 minutes. Reduce oven
temperature to 350°; continue baking 35
to 40 minutes or until knife inserted
near center comes out clean. Cool.
Garnish as desired. Refrigerate
leftovers.

MAI TAI PIE

Makes one 9-inch pie

Coconut Crust
1 (8-ounce) package cream cheese,
 softened
1 (14-ounce) can Eagle® Brand
 Sweetened Condensed Milk
 (NOT evaporated milk)
1 (6-ounce) can frozen orange juice
 concentrate, thawed
¼ cup light rum
2 tablespoons orange-flavored
 liqueur
1 cup (½ pint) Borden® Whipping
 Cream, whipped
Orange slices, optional

Prepare Coconut Crust. In large mixer
bowl, beat cheese until fluffy. Gradually
beat in sweetened condensed milk, then
juice concentrate until smooth. Stir in
rum and liqueur. Fold in whipped
cream. Pour into prepared crust. Freeze
4 hours or chill at least 3 hours. Garnish
with orange slices if desired. Refrigerate
or freeze leftovers.

Coconut Crust: Preheat oven to 325°. In
medium bowl, combine 1 (7-ounce)
package flaked coconut (2⅔ cups) and 3
tablespoons margarine or butter, melted.
Press firmly on bottom and up side to
rim of 9-inch pie plate. Bake 20 minutes
or until golden brown. Cool.

APPLE CRANBERRY STREUSEL CUSTARD PIE

Makes one 9-inch pie

1 (9-inch) unbaked pastry shell
1 (14-ounce) can Eagle® Brand
 Sweetened Condensed Milk
 (NOT evaporated milk)
1 teaspoon ground cinnamon
2 eggs, beaten
½ cup hot water
1½ cups fresh or dry-pack frozen
 cranberries
2 medium all-purpose apples, peeled
 and sliced (about 1½ cups)
½ cup firmly packed brown sugar
½ cup unsifted flour
¼ cup cold margarine or butter
½ cup chopped nuts

Place rack in lower third of oven;
preheat oven to 425°. In large bowl,
combine sweetened condensed milk and
cinnamon. Add eggs, water and fruits;
mix well. Pour into pastry shell. In
medium bowl, combine sugar and flour;
cut in margarine until crumbly. Add
nuts. Sprinkle over pie. Bake 10
minutes. Reduce oven temperature to
375°; continue baking 30 to 40 minutes
or until golden brown. Cool. Refrigerate
leftovers.

BANANA CREAM CHEESE PIE ▲

Makes one 9-inch pie

1 (9-inch) graham cracker crumb crust
  or baked pastry shell
1 (8-ounce) package cream cheese,
  softened
1 (14-ounce) can Eagle® Brand
  Sweetened Condensed Milk
  (NOT evaporated milk)
⅓ cup ReaLemon® Lemon Juice from
  Concentrate
1 teaspoon vanilla extract
4 medium bananas
  Additional ReaLemon® brand

In large mixer bowl, beat cheese until
fluffy. Gradually beat in sweetened
condensed milk until smooth. Stir in ⅓
cup ReaLemon® brand and vanilla. Slice
2 bananas; dip in ReaLemon® brand.
Drain and line crust with bananas. Pour
filling over bananas; cover. Chill 3 hours
or until set. Before serving, slice
remaining 2 bananas; dip in ReaLemon®
brand. Drain; arrange bananas on top of
pie. Refrigerate leftovers.

WALNUT TRUFFLE PIE

Makes one 9-inch pie

1 (9-inch) unbaked pastry shell
1 (6-ounce) package semi-sweet
  chocolate chips
¼ cup margarine or butter
1 (14-ounce) can Eagle® Brand
  Sweetened Condensed Milk
  (NOT evaporated milk)
1 cup coarsely chopped walnuts
3 eggs, well beaten
3 tablespoons rum or 1½ teaspoons
  rum flavoring, optional
½ teaspoon instant coffee

Place rack in lower third of oven;
preheat oven to 400°. In medium
saucepan, over low heat, melt chips
with margarine. Remove from heat; stir
in remaining ingredients except pastry
shell; mix well. Pour into pastry shell.
Bake 10 minutes. Reduce oven
temperature to 350°; continue baking 25
minutes or until center is set. Cool.
Serve chilled with whipped cream if
desired. Refrigerate leftovers.

CITRUS ANGEL TARTS

Makes 10 tarts

10 (3-inch) Meringue Shells
3 egg yolks*
1 (14-ounce) can Eagle® Brand Sweetened Condensed Milk (NOT evaporated milk)
½ cup ReaLemon® Lemon Juice from Concentrate
2 teaspoons grated orange rind
Few drops yellow food coloring, optional
1 cup (½ pint) Borden® Whipping Cream, whipped

Prepare Meringue Shells; set aside. In medium bowl, beat egg yolks; stir in sweetened condensed milk, ReaLemon® brand, rind and food coloring if desired. Fold in whipped cream. Chill at least 2 hours. Just before serving, spoon equal portions into Meringue Shells. Garnish as desired. Refrigerate leftovers.

Meringue Shells: Cover baking sheets with ungreased brown paper. On paper, draw 10 (3-inch) circles about 2 inches apart; set aside. Preheat oven to 300°. In large mixer bowl, combine 3 egg whites at room temperature, 1 teaspoon vanilla extract, ½ teaspoon cream of tartar and dash salt. On medium speed, beat until soft peaks form. On high speed, gradually beat in 1 cup sugar until very stiff peaks form. Stir in ¾ cup finely chopped nuts. Spread each of the small circles on paper with about ⅓ cup meringue, using spoon to shape into shells *or* pipe through a pastry tube. Bake 35 to 40 minutes or until a light beige color. Cool.

*Use only Grade A clean, uncracked eggs.

HAWAIIAN CHEESE PIE

Makes one 9-inch pie

2½ cups flaked coconut, lightly toasted
⅓ cup margarine or butter, melted
1 (8-ounce) package cream cheese, softened
1 (14-ounce) can Eagle® Brand Sweetened Condensed Milk (NOT evaporated milk)
⅓ cup frozen orange juice concentrate, thawed
1 (8-ounce) can crushed pineapple, *well drained*
1½ teaspoons grated orange rind
Yellow food coloring, optional
1 (8-ounce) container frozen non-dairy whipped topping, thawed

Preheat oven to 400°. Combine coconut and margarine; press on bottom and up side to rim of 9-inch pie plate. Bake 4 to 5 minutes. Cool. In large mixer bowl, beat cheese until fluffy. Gradually beat in sweetened condensed milk until smooth, then juice concentrate. Stir in pineapple, rind and food coloring if desired. Fold in whipped topping. Chill 3 hours or until set. Garnish as desired. Refrigerate leftovers.

HAWAIIAN CHEESE PIE

CHOCOLATE MOUSSE TARTS

Makes 12 tarts

1 (14-ounce) can Eagle® Brand
    Sweetened Condensed Milk
    (NOT evaporated milk)
1 (4-serving size) package *instant*
    chocolate flavor pudding mix
¼ cup unsweetened cocoa
¼ cup cold water
1 cup (½ pint) Borden® Whipping
    Cream, whipped
12 (3-inch) prepared tart-size crusts

In large mixer bowl, beat sweetened condensed milk, pudding mix, cocoa and water until smooth and well blended; chill 5 minutes. Fold in whipped cream. Spoon equal portions into crusts. Chill. Garnish as desired. Refrigerate leftovers.

Chocolate Brandy Mousse Tarts: Reduce water to 2 tablespoons; add 2 tablespoons brandy. Proceed as above.

ORANGE BLOSSOM PIE

Makes 1 pie

1 (14-ounce) can Eagle® Brand
    Sweetened Condensed Milk
    (NOT evaporated milk)
4 egg yolks
½ cup orange juice
1 tablespoon grated orange rind
1 (6-ounce) packaged graham cracker
    crumb pie crust
1 (3-ounce) package cream cheese,
    softened
⅓ cup confectioners' sugar
¼ cup Borden® Sour Cream
¼ teaspoon vanilla extract

Preheat oven to 325°. In large bowl, combine sweetened condensed milk, egg yolks, orange juice and rind; mix well. Pour into crust (mixture will be thin). Bake 35 minutes or until knife inserted near center comes out clean. Meanwhile, in small mixer bowl, combine remaining ingredients; beat until smooth. Spread evenly over pie. Bake 10 minutes longer. Cool. Chill. Garnish as desired. Refrigerate leftovers.

MINCE LIME PIE

Makes one 9-inch pie

1 (9-inch) baked pastry shell
1 (14-ounce) can Eagle® Brand
    Sweetened Condensed Milk
    (NOT evaporated milk)
2 eggs
1⅓ cups (one-half jar) None Such®
    Ready-to-Use Mincemeat
    (Regular *or* Brandy & Rum)
⅓ cup ReaLime® Lime Juice from
    Concentrate
¼ teaspoon grated lime rind, optional
⅛ teaspoon salt
1 (8-ounce) container Borden® Sour
    Cream
2 tablespoons sugar
½ teaspoon vanilla extract

Preheat oven to 350°. In large mixer bowl, beat sweetened condensed milk and eggs. Stir in *1 cup* mincemeat, ReaLime® brand, rind if desired and salt. Pour into prepared pastry shell; bake 15 minutes. Meanwhile, in small bowl, combine sour cream, sugar and vanilla. Spread evenly over pie. Return to oven; bake 10 minutes. Cool. Chill 3 to 4 hours. Garnish with remaining *⅓ cup* mincemeat before serving. Refrigerate leftovers.

RASPBERRY-TOPPED LEMON PIE

Makes 1 pie

1 (10-ounce) package frozen red
   raspberries in syrup, thawed
1 tablespoon cornstarch
3 egg yolks*
1 (14-ounce) can Eagle® Brand
   Sweetened Condensed Milk
   (NOT evaporated milk)
½ cup ReaLemon® Lemon Juice from
   Concentrate
   Yellow food coloring, optional
1 (6-ounce) packaged graham cracker
   crumb pie crust
   Whipped topping

Preheat oven to 350°. In small saucepan, combine raspberries and cornstarch; cook and stir until mixture thickens and is clear. In medium bowl, beat egg yolks; stir in sweetened condensed milk, ReaLemon® brand and food coloring if desired. Pour into crust; bake 8 minutes. Spoon raspberry mixture evenly over top. Chill 4 hours or until set. Top with whipped topping. Garnish as desired. Refrigerate leftovers.

*Use only Grade A clean, uncracked eggs.

KEY LIME PIE

Makes one 9- or 10-inch pie

1 (9- or 10-inch) baked pastry shell *or* graham cracker crumb crust*
6 egg yolks**
2 (14-ounce) cans Eagle® Brand Sweetened Condensed Milk (NOT evaporated milk)
1 (8-ounce) bottle ReaLime® Lime Juice from Concentrate
1 to 2 drops green food coloring, optional
Whipped cream or whipped topping

Preheat oven to 350°. In large mixer bowl, beat egg yolks with sweetened condensed milk. Stir in ReaLime® brand and food coloring if desired. Pour into prepared pastry shell; bake 12 minutes. Cool. Chill. Top with whipped cream. Garnish as desired. Refrigerate leftovers.

Key Lime Meringue Pie: Omit whipped cream. Prepare filling as above, reserving 4 egg whites; do not bake filling. In small mixer bowl, beat egg whites with ¼ teaspoon cream of tartar until soft peaks form; gradually add ½ cup sugar, beating until stiff but not dry. Spread on top of pie, sealing carefully to edge of pastry shell. Bake in preheated 350° oven 15 minutes or until lightly browned. Cool. Chill.

*If using frozen packaged pie shell or 6-ounce packaged graham cracker crumb pie crust, use 1 can Eagle® Brand Sweetened Condensed Milk, 3 egg yolks and ½ cup ReaLime® brand. Bake 8 minutes. Proceed as above.

**Use only Grade A clean, uncracked eggs.

NO-BAKE BLUEBERRY CHEESE PIE

Makes one 9-inch pie

1 (9-inch) graham cracker crumb crust *or* baked pastry shell
1 (8-ounce) package cream cheese, softened
1 (14-ounce) can Eagle® Brand Sweetened Condensed Milk (NOT evaporated milk)
⅓ cup plus 2 tablespoons ReaLemon® Lemon Juice from Concentrate
1 teaspoon vanilla extract
¼ cup sugar
1 tablespoon cornstarch
½ cup water
2 cups fresh or dry-pack frozen blueberries, rinsed and sorted

In large mixer bowl, beat cheese until fluffy. Gradually beat in sweetened condensed milk until smooth. Stir in ⅓ *cup* ReaLemon® brand and vanilla. Pour into prepared crust. In medium saucepan, combine sugar and cornstarch; mix well. Add water and remaining *2 tablespoons* ReaLemon® brand, then blueberries. Bring to a boil; reduce heat and simmer 3 minutes or until thick and clear. Cool 10 minutes. Spread over pie. Chill 3 hours or until set. Refrigerate leftovers.

NO-BAKE PUMPKIN PIE

Makes 1 pie

1 egg
1 (14-ounce) can Eagle® Brand Sweetened Condensed Milk (NOT evaporated milk)
1 teaspoon ground cinnamon
½ teaspoon ground ginger
½ teaspoon ground nutmeg
½ teaspoon salt
1 envelope unflavored gelatine
2 tablespoons water
1 (16-ounce) can pumpkin (2 cups)
1 (6-ounce) packaged graham cracker crumb pie crust

In medium bowl, beat egg; beat in sweetened condensed milk, spices and salt. In medium saucepan, sprinkle gelatine over water; let stand 1 minute. Over *low* heat, stir until gelatine dissolves. Add sweetened condensed milk mixture; over *low* heat, cook and stir constantly until mixture thickens slightly, 5 to 10 minutes. Remove from heat. Stir in pumpkin. Pour into crust. Chill 4 hours or until set. Garnish as desired. Refrigerate leftovers.

NO-BAKE PUMPKIN PIE

CREAMY CHOCOLATE PIE

Makes one 9-inch pie

1 (9-inch) baked pastry shell
3 (1-ounce) squares unsweetened *or* semi-sweet chocolate
1 (14-ounce) can Eagle® Brand Sweetened Condensed Milk (NOT evaporated milk)
¼ teaspoon salt
¼ cup hot water
1 teaspoon vanilla extract
1 cup (½ pint) Borden® Whipping Cream
   Additional whipped cream or whipped topping
   Shaved chocolate

In heavy saucepan, over medium heat, melt chocolate with sweetened condensed milk and salt. Cook and stir until *very thick* and fudgy, 5 to 8 minutes. Add water; cook and stir until thickened and bubbly. Remove from heat; add vanilla. Cool 15 minutes. *Chill thoroughly*, 20 to 30 minutes; stir. In large mixer bowl, beat *1 cup* whipping cream until stiff; fold into cooled chocolate mixture. Pour into prepared pastry shell. Chill 3 hours or until set. Garnish with additional whipped cream and shaved chocolate. Refrigerate leftovers.

BLUEBERRY STREUSEL COBBLER

Makes 6 to 8 servings

1 pint fresh or dry-pack frozen blueberries, rinsed and sorted
1 (14-ounce) can Eagle® Brand Sweetened Condensed Milk (NOT evaporated milk)
2 teaspoons grated lemon rind
¾ cup plus 2 tablespoons cold margarine or butter
2 cups biscuit baking mix
½ cup firmly packed brown sugar
½ cup chopped nuts

Preheat oven to 325°. In medium bowl, combine blueberries, sweetened condensed milk and rind. In large bowl, cut ¾ cup margarine into 1½ cups biscuit mix until crumbly. Stir in blueberry mixture. Spread in greased 9-inch square baking pan. In small bowl, combine remaining ½ cup biscuit mix and sugar; cut in remaining 2 *tablespoons* margarine until crumbly. Stir in nuts. Sprinkle evenly over cobbler. Bake 1 hour to 1 hour and 10 minutes or until golden brown. Serve warm with vanilla ice cream if desired.

LUSCIOUS SWEET POTATO PIE

Makes one 9-inch pie

1 (9-inch) unbaked pastry shell
1 pound (2 medium) sweet potatoes or yams, cooked and peeled
½ cup margarine or butter, softened
1 (14-ounce) can Eagle® Brand Sweetened Condensed Milk (NOT evaporated milk)
¼ cup orange-flavored liqueur *or* 2 teaspoons grated orange rind
1 teaspoon ground cinnamon
½ teaspoon ground nutmeg
¼ teaspoon salt
2 eggs, beaten

Preheat oven to 350°. In large mixer bowl, mash sweet potatoes with margarine; add remaining ingredients except pastry shell and eggs. Beat until smooth and well blended. Stir in eggs. Pour into pastry shell. Bake 50 to 55 minutes or until knife inserted near center comes out clean. Cool. Refrigerate leftovers.

Tip: 1 (16- or 17-ounce) can sweet potatoes or yams, drained, can be substituted for fresh. Melt margarine. Proceed as above.

QUICK LIME CREAM PIE

Makes 1 pie

1 (14-ounce) can Eagle® Brand
  Sweetened Condensed Milk
  (NOT evaporated milk)
½ cup ReaLime® Lime Juice from
  Concentrate
  Green food coloring, optional
1 cup (½ pint) Borden® Whipping
  Cream, whipped
1 (6-ounce) packaged graham cracker
  crumb pie crust

In medium bowl, stir together
sweetened condensed milk, ReaLime®
brand and food coloring if desired. Fold
in whipped cream. Pour into crust. Chill
3 hours or until set. Garnish as desired.
Refrigerate leftovers.

Quick Lemon Cream Pie: Substitute
½ cup ReaLemon® Lemon Juice from
Concentrate for ReaLime® brand.

LIME DAIQUIRI PIE

Makes one 9-inch pie

1 (9-inch) baked pastry shell
1 (8-ounce) package cream cheese, softened
1 (14-ounce) can Eagle® Brand Sweetened Condensed Milk (NOT evaporated milk)
⅓ cup ReaLime® Lime Juice from Concentrate
2 tablespoons white rum *or*
   ¾ teaspoon rum flavoring
2 to 3 drops green food coloring, optional
1 cup (½ pint) Borden® Whipping Cream, whipped
   Additional whipped cream, optional
   Lime slices, optional

In large mixer bowl, beat cheese until fluffy. Gradually beat in sweetened condensed milk until smooth. Stir in ReaLime® brand, rum and food coloring if desired. Fold in whipped cream. Pour into prepared crust. Chill 2 hours or until set. Garnish with additional whipped cream and lime slices if desired. Refrigerate leftovers.

LEMON CHIFFON PIE

Makes one 9-inch pie

1 (9-inch) graham cracker crumb crust *or* baked pastry shell
1 (14-ounce) can Eagle® Brand Sweetened Condensed Milk (NOT evaporated milk)
⅓ cup ReaLemon® Lemon Juice from Concentrate
   Few drops yellow food coloring, optional
3 egg whites*
¼ teaspoon cream of tartar

In medium bowl, combine sweetened condensed milk, ReaLemon® brand and food coloring if desired. In small mixer bowl, beat egg whites with cream of tartar until stiff but not dry; gently fold into sweetened condensed milk mixture. Pour into prepared crust. Chill 3 hours or until set. Refrigerate leftovers.

*Use only Grade A clean, uncracked eggs.

AMBROSIA PIE

Makes one 9-inch pie

2 cups flaked coconut
3 tablespoons margarine or butter, melted
1 (14-ounce) can Eagle® Brand Sweetened Condensed Milk (NOT evaporated milk)
⅓ cup ReaLemon® Lemon Juice from Concentrate
1 (15¼-ounce) can crushed pineapple, well drained
1 large orange, peeled and cut into bite-size pieces
   Dash ground ginger
½ cup slivered almonds, toasted and chopped
1 cup (½ pint) Borden® Whipping Cream, whipped
   Additional fresh fruit, optional

Preheat oven to 350°. Combine coconut and margarine. Reserving 2 *tablespoons* coconut mixture, press remainder firmly on bottom and up side to rim of 9-inch pie plate. Bake 12 minutes or until edge is golden. Cool. Toast reserved coconut mixture. In large bowl, combine sweetened condensed milk, ReaLemon® brand, pineapple, orange and ginger. Fold in almonds and whipped cream. Pour into prepared crust. Garnish with reserved coconut and additional fruit if desired. Chill 4 hours or until set. Refrigerate leftovers.

Left: Cool and Minty Party Cake. Right: New York Style Marbled Cheesecake (recipes, page 52)

CAKES &
CHEESECAKES

COOL AND MINTY PARTY CAKE

Makes one 9-inch cake

1 (14-ounce) can Eagle® Brand
Sweetened Condensed Milk
(NOT evaporated milk)
2 teaspoons peppermint extract
8 drops green food coloring
2 cups (1 pint) Borden® Whipping
Cream, whipped (*do not use non-
dairy whipped topping*)
1 (18¼- or 18½-ounce) package
yellow or white cake mix
Green creme de menthe
1 (8-ounce) container frozen non-
dairy whipped topping, thawed

In large bowl, combine sweetened
condensed milk, extract and food
coloring. Fold in whipped cream. Pour
into aluminum foil-lined 9-inch round
layer cake pan; cover. Freeze 6 hours or
until firm. Meanwhile, prepare and
bake cake mix as package directs for two
9-inch round layers. Remove from pans;
cool thoroughly. With fork, poke holes
in layers 1 inch apart halfway through
each layer. Spoon small amounts of
creme de menthe in holes. Place 1 cake
layer on serving plate; top with ice
cream layer then second cake layer. Trim
ice cream layer to edge of cake layers.
Frost quickly with whipped topping.
Return to freezer at least 6 hours before
serving. Garnish as desired. Return
leftovers to freezer.

Tip: Cake can be made 1 week ahead
and stored, tightly wrapped, in freezer.

NEW YORK STYLE MARBLED CHEESECAKE

Makes one 9-inch cheesecake

1¼ cups graham cracker crumbs
¼ cup sugar
⅓ cup margarine or butter, melted
4 (8-ounce) packages cream cheese,
softened
1 (14-ounce) can Eagle® Brand
Sweetened Condensed Milk
(NOT evaporated milk)
4 eggs
⅓ cup unsifted flour
1 tablespoon vanilla extract
2 to 4 (1-ounce) squares semi-sweet
chocolate, melted

Preheat oven to 350°. Combine crumbs,
sugar and margarine; press firmly on
bottom of 9-inch springform pan. In
large mixer bowl, beat cheese until
fluffy. Gradually beat in sweetened
condensed milk until smooth. Beat in
eggs then flour and vanilla. Measure 1½
cups batter into medium bowl. Add
melted chocolate; mix well. Spoon half
the yellow batter into prepared pan,
then half the chocolate batter. Repeat,
ending with chocolate batter. With metal
spatula, cut through batter to marble
cake. Bake 1 hour or until lightly
browned around edge. Cool to room
temperature. Chill. Garnish as desired.
Refrigerate leftovers.

Tip: For best marbled effect, do not
oversoften or overbeat cream cheese.

CHOCOLATE SHEET CAKE

Makes one 15×10-inch cake

1¼ cups margarine or butter
½ cup unsweetened cocoa
1 cup water
2 cups unsifted flour
1½ cups firmly packed brown sugar
1 teaspoon baking soda
1 teaspoon ground cinnamon
½ teaspoon salt
1 (14-ounce) can Eagle® Brand
    Sweetened Condensed Milk
    (NOT evaporated milk)
2 eggs
1 teaspoon vanilla extract
1 cup confectioners' sugar
1 cup coarsely chopped nuts

Preheat oven to 350°. In small saucepan, melt *1 cup* margarine; stir in *¼ cup* cocoa, then water. Bring to a boil; remove from heat. In large mixer bowl, combine flour, brown sugar, baking soda, cinnamon and salt. Add cocoa mixture; beat well. Stir in *⅓ cup* sweetened condensed milk, eggs and vanilla. Pour into greased 15×10-inch jellyroll pan. Bake 15 minutes or until cake springs back when lightly touched. In small saucepan, melt remaining *¼ cup* margarine; add remaining *¼ cup* cocoa and remaining sweetened condensed milk. Stir in confectioners' sugar and nuts. Spread on *warm* cake.

Chocolate Mocha Sheet Cake: Add 1 tablespoon instant coffee with cocoa to cake; add 1 tablespoon instant coffee with cocoa to frosting.

LUSCIOUS BAKED CHOCOLATE CHEESECAKE

Makes one 9-inch cheesecake

1¼ cups graham cracker crumbs
¼ cup sugar
⅓ cup margarine or butter, melted
3 (8-ounce) packages cream cheese, softened
1 (14-ounce) can Eagle® Brand Sweetened Condensed Milk (NOT evaporated milk)
1 (12-ounce) package semi-sweet chocolate chips *or* 8 (1-ounce) squares semi-sweet chocolate, melted
4 eggs
2 teaspoons vanilla extract

Preheat oven to 300°. Combine crumbs, sugar and margarine; press firmly on bottom of 9-inch springform pan. In large mixer bowl, beat cheese until fluffy. Gradually beat in sweetened condensed milk until smooth. Add remaining ingredients; mix well. Pour into prepared pan. Bake 1 hour and 5 minutes or until set. Cool. Chill. Garnish as desired. Refrigerate leftovers.

CHOCOLATE CHIP CHEESECAKE

Makes one 9-inch cheesecake

1½ cups finely crushed creme-filled chocolate sandwich cookies (about 18 cookies)
2 to 3 tablespoons margarine or butter, melted
3 (8-ounce) packages cream cheese, softened
1 (14-ounce) can Eagle® Brand Sweetened Condensed Milk (NOT evaporated milk)
3 eggs
2 teaspoons vanilla extract
1 cup mini chocolate chips
1 teaspoon flour

Preheat oven to 300°. Combine crumbs and margarine; press firmly on bottom of 9-inch springform pan *or* 13×9-inch baking pan. In large mixer bowl, beat cheese until fluffy. Gradually beat in sweetened condensed milk until smooth. Add eggs and vanilla; mix well. In small bowl, toss together ½ *cup* chips with flour to coat; stir into cheese mixture. Pour into prepared pan. Sprinkle remaining chips evenly over top. Bake 55 to 60 minutes or until set. Cool. Chill. Garnish as desired. Refrigerate leftovers.

Mint Chocolate Chip Cheesecake: Prepare crust as above. Add ½ to 1 teaspoon peppermint extract and if desired ⅛ to ¼ teaspoon green food coloring to cream cheese mixture. Proceed as above.

Tip: For best distribution of chips throughout cheesecake, do not oversoften or overbeat cream cheese.

LUSCIOUS BAKED CHOCOLATE CHEESECAKE (TOP), CHOCOLATE CHIP CHEESECAKE (BOTTOM)

CREAMY BAKED CHEESECAKE

Makes one 9-inch cheesecake

1¼ cups graham cracker crumbs
¼ cup sugar
⅓ cup margarine or butter, melted
2 (8-ounce) packages cream cheese, softened
1 (14-ounce) can Eagle® Brand Sweetened Condensed Milk (NOT evaporated milk)
3 eggs
¼ cup ReaLemon® Lemon Juice from Concentrate
1 (8-ounce) container Borden® Sour Cream
Raspberry Topping, optional

Preheat oven to 300°. Combine crumbs, sugar and margarine; press firmly on bottom of 9-inch springform pan. In large mixer bowl, beat cheese until fluffy. Gradually beat in sweetened condensed milk until smooth. Add eggs and ReaLemon® brand; mix well. Pour into prepared pan. Bake 50 to 55 minutes or until set; top with sour cream. Bake 5 minutes longer. Cool. Chill. Serve with Raspberry Topping if desired. Refrigerate leftovers.

Raspberry Topping: In small saucepan, combine ⅔ cup syrup drained from 1 (10-ounce) package thawed frozen red raspberries, ¼ cup red currant jelly or red raspberry jam and 1 tablespoon cornstarch. Cook and stir until slightly thickened and clear. Cool. Add raspberries. If desired, drain 1 (16-ounce) can peach slices; arrange on cake. Top with sauce.

NO-BAKE PEACH CHEESECAKE

Makes one 9-inch cheesecake

1¼ cups graham cracker crumbs
¼ cup sugar
⅓ cup margarine or butter, melted
1 (29-ounce) can peach halves, drained, reserving syrup
1 envelope unflavored gelatine
2 (8-ounce) packages cream cheese, softened
1 (14-ounce) can Eagle® Brand Sweetened Condensed Milk (NOT evaporated milk)
2 tablespoons ReaLemon® Lemon Juice from Concentrate
1 (4-ounce) container frozen non-dairy whipped topping, thawed

Combine crumbs, sugar and margarine. Reserving 2 tablespoons crumbs, press remainder firmly on bottom of 9-inch springform pan *or* 13×9-inch baking pan. In small saucepan, sprinkle gelatine over ½ *cup* reserved syrup; let stand 1 minute. Over low heat, stir until gelatine dissolves. Slice 2 peach halves for garnish; reserve. In blender container, puree remaining peaches; combine with gelatine mixture. In large mixer bowl, beat cheese until fluffy. Gradually beat in sweetened condensed milk until smooth. Stir in ReaLemon® brand and peach mixture. Fold in whipped topping; pour into prepared pan. Chill 3 hours or until set. Garnish with reserved crumbs and peach slices. Refrigerate leftovers.

NO-BAKE CHOCOLATE CHEESECAKE

Makes one 9-inch cheesecake

1¼ cups graham cracker crumbs
¼ cup sugar
⅓ cup margarine or butter, melted
1 envelope unflavored gelatine
⅔ cup water
2 (8-ounce) packages cream cheese, softened
4 (1-ounce) squares semi-sweet chocolate, melted
1 (14-ounce) can Eagle® Brand Sweetened Condensed Milk (NOT evaporated milk)
1 teaspoon vanilla extract
1 cup (½ pint) Borden® Whipping Cream, whipped

Combine crumbs, sugar and margarine; press firmly on bottom of 9-inch springform pan. In small saucepan, sprinkle gelatine over water; let stand 1 minute. Over low heat, stir until gelatine dissolves. In large mixer bowl, beat cheese and chocolate until fluffy. Gradually beat in sweetened condensed milk and vanilla until smooth. Stir in gelatine mixture. Fold in whipped cream. Pour into prepared pan. Chill 3 hours or until set. Garnish as desired. Refrigerate leftovers.

EVER-SO-EASY FRUITCAKE

Makes two 9×5-inch loaves

2½ cups unsifted flour
1 teaspoon baking soda
2 eggs, slightly beaten
1 jar None Such® Ready-to-Use Mincemeat (Regular *or* Brandy & Rum)
1 (14-ounce) can Eagle® Brand Sweetened Condensed Milk (NOT evaporated milk)
2 cups (1 pound) mixed candied fruit
1 cup coarsely chopped nuts

Preheat oven to 300°. Grease two 9×5-inch loaf pans. Combine flour and baking soda. In large bowl, combine remaining ingredients; stir in flour mixture. Pour half the batter into each prepared pan. Bake 1 hour and 20 to 25 minutes or until wooden pick inserted near center comes out clean. Cool 15 minutes. Turn out of pans. Cool. Glaze and garnish as desired.

Fruitcake Bars: Grease 15×10-inch jellyroll pan; spread batter evenly in pan. Bake 40 to 45 minutes. Cool. Glaze if desired. (Makes about 4 dozen bars)

Fruitcake-in-a-Can: Grease three 1-pound coffee cans; fill each can with about 2⅔ cups batter. Bake 1 hour and 20 to 25 minutes. *Or,* grease eight 10¾-ounce soup cans; fill each with 1 cup batter. Bake 50 to 55 minutes.

Bundt Fruitcake: Generously grease and flour 10-inch bundt pan; turn batter into pan. Bake 1 hour and 45 to 50 minutes.

Fruitcake Mini Loaves: Grease twelve 2½×4½-inch loaf pans. Fill each pan ⅔ full. Bake 35 to 40 minutes.

Fruitcake Cookies: Drop by rounded tablespoonfuls, 2 inches apart, onto greased baking sheets. Bake 15 to 18 minutes. (Makes about 5½ dozen cookies)

Tip: To substitute condensed mincemeat for ready-to-use mincemeat, crumble 2 (9-ounce) packages None Such® Condensed Mincemeat into small saucepan; add 1½ cups water. Boil briskly 1 minute. Cool. Proceed as above.

ALMOND CHEESECAKE

Makes one 9-inch cheesecake

¾ cup graham cracker crumbs
½ cup slivered almonds, toasted and finely chopped
¼ cup sugar
¼ cup margarine or butter, melted
3 (8-ounce) packages cream cheese, softened
1 (14-ounce) can Eagle® Brand Sweetened Condensed Milk (NOT evaporated milk)
3 eggs
1 teaspoon almond extract
Almond Praline Topping

Preheat oven to 300°. Combine crumbs, almonds, sugar and margarine; press firmly on bottom of 9-inch springform pan *or* 13×9-inch baking pan. In large mixer bowl, beat cheese until fluffy. Gradually beat in sweetened condensed milk until smooth. Add eggs and extract; mix well. Pour into prepared pan. Bake 55 to 60 minutes or until set. Cool. Top with Almond Praline Topping. Chill. Refrigerate leftovers.

Almond Praline Topping: In small saucepan, combine ⅓ cup firmly packed dark brown sugar and ⅓ cup Borden® Whipping Cream. Cook and stir until sugar dissolves. Simmer 5 minutes. Remove from heat; stir in ½ cup chopped toasted slivered almonds. Spoon evenly over cake. (For 13×9-inch pan, double all topping ingredients; simmer 10 to 12 minutes.)

Cakes & Cheesecakes 59

CREAMY FRUIT 'N' NUT CHEESECAKE▲

Makes one 9-inch cheesecake

1¼ cups graham cracker crumbs

¼ cup sugar

⅓ cup margarine or butter, melted

2 (8-ounce) packages cream cheese, softened

1 (14-ounce) can Eagle® Brand Sweetened Condensed Milk (NOT evaporated milk)

1 envelope unflavored gelatine

¼ cup ReaLemon® Lemon Juice from Concentrate

1⅓ cups (one-half jar) None Such® Ready-to-Use Mincemeat

½ cup chopped nuts

1 tablespoon grated lemon rind

1 cup (½ pint) Borden® Whipping Cream, whipped

Sour cream and additional nuts, optional

Combine crumbs, sugar and margarine; press firmly on bottom of 9-inch springform pan. In large mixer bowl, beat cheese until fluffy. Gradually beat in sweetened condensed milk until smooth. In small saucepan, sprinkle gelatine over ReaLemon® brand; let stand 1 minute. Over low heat, stir until gelatine dissolves. Add to cheese mixture with mincemeat, nuts and rind; mix well. Fold in whipped cream; pour into prepared pan. Chill 3 hours or until set. Garnish with sour cream and additional nuts if desired. Refrigerate leftovers.

LEMON CREAM CHEESE FROSTING

Makes about 4 cups

1 (8-ounce) package cream cheese, softened
1 (14-ounce) can Eagle® Brand Sweetened Condensed Milk (NOT evaporated milk)
⅓ cup ReaLemon® Lemon Juice from Concentrate
1 teaspoon vanilla extract
1 (4-ounce) container frozen non-dairy whipped topping, thawed

In large mixer bowl, beat cheese until fluffy. Gradually beat in sweetened condensed milk until smooth. Stir in ReaLemon® brand and vanilla. Fold in whipped topping. Chill at least 1 hour to thicken. Use to frost 4 dozen cupcakes or one (15×10-inch) sheet cake. Store in refrigerator.

CHOCOLATE ALMOND TORTE

Makes one 4-layer cake

4 eggs, separated
½ cup margarine or butter, softened
1 cup sugar
1 teaspoon vanilla extract
1 teaspoon almond extract
1 cup finely chopped toasted almonds
¾ cup unsifted flour
½ cup unsweetened cocoa
½ teaspoon baking powder
½ teaspoon baking soda
⅔ cup Borden® Milk
Chocolate Almond Frosting

Preheat oven to 350°. In small mixer bowl, beat egg whites until soft peaks form; set aside. In large mixer bowl, beat margarine and sugar until fluffy. Add egg yolks and extracts; mix well. Stir together almonds, flour, cocoa, baking powder and baking soda; add alternately with milk to sugar mixture, beating well after each addition. Fold in beaten egg whites. Pour into two waxed paper-lined ungreased 8- or 9-inch round layer cake pans. Bake 18 to 20 minutes or until wooden pick inserted near center comes out clean. Cool 10 minutes; remove from pans. Cool thoroughly. Split each cake layer; fill and frost cake with Chocolate Almond Frosting. Chill several hours. Garnish as desired. Refrigerate leftovers.

Chocolate Almond Frosting: In heavy saucepan, over medium heat, melt 2 (1-ounce) squares semi-sweet chocolate with 1 (14-ounce) can Eagle® Brand Sweetened Condensed Milk (NOT evaporated milk). Cook and stir until mixture thickens, about 10 minutes. Remove from heat; cool 10 minutes. Stir in 1 teaspoon almond extract; cool. (Makes about 1½ cups)

STRAWBERRY TUNNEL CREAM CAKE

Makes one 10-inch cake

1 (10-inch) prepared round angel food cake
2 (3-ounce) packages cream cheese, softened
1 (14-ounce) can Eagle® Brand Sweetened Condensed Milk (NOT evaporated milk)
⅓ cup ReaLemon® Lemon Juice from Concentrate
1 teaspoon almond extract
2 to 4 drops red food coloring, optional
1 cup chopped fresh strawberries *or* 1 (16-ounce) package frozen strawberries, thawed and well drained
1 (12-ounce) container frozen non-dairy whipped topping, thawed
Additional fresh strawberries, optional

Invert cake onto serving plate. Cut 1-inch slice crosswise from top of cake; set aside. With sharp knife, cut around cake 1 inch from center hole and 1 inch from outer edge, leaving cake walls 1-inch thick. Remove cake from center, leaving 1-inch thick base on bottom of cake. Tear cake removed from center into bite-size pieces; reserve. In large mixer bowl, beat cheese until fluffy. Gradually beat in sweetened condensed milk until smooth. Stir in ReaLemon® brand, extract and food coloring if desired. Stir in reserved cake pieces and chopped strawberries. Fold in *1 cup* whipped topping. Fill cake cavity with strawberry mixture; replace top slice of cake. Frost with remaining whipped topping. Chill 3 hours or freeze 4 hours. Garnish with strawberries if desired. Return leftovers to refrigerator or freezer.

WALNUT RUM RAISIN CHEESECAKE

Makes one 9-inch cheesecake

1 cup raisins
2 tablespoons rum *or* water plus ½ teaspoon rum flavoring
1 cup graham cracker crumbs
½ cup finely chopped walnuts
¼ cup sugar
¼ cup margarine or butter, melted
3 (8-ounce) packages cream cheese, softened
1 (14-ounce) can Eagle® Brand Sweetened Condensed Milk (NOT evaporated milk)
3 eggs
Walnut Praline Glaze

Preheat oven to 300°. In small bowl, combine raisins and rum; set aside. Combine crumbs, walnuts, sugar and margarine; press firmly on bottom of 9-inch springform pan *or* 13×9-inch baking pan. In large mixer bowl, beat cheese until fluffy. Gradually beat in sweetened condensed milk until smooth. Add eggs; mix well. Drain rum from raisins; stir rum into batter. Pour into prepared pan. Top evenly with raisins. Bake 55 to 60 minutes or until set. Cool. Top with Walnut Praline Glaze. Chill. Refrigerate leftovers.

Walnut Praline Glaze: In small saucepan, combine ⅓ cup firmly packed dark brown sugar and ⅓ cup Borden® Whipping Cream. Cook and stir until sugar dissolves. Bring to a boil; reduce heat and simmer 5 minutes. Remove from heat; stir in ¾ cup chopped toasted walnuts. Spoon over cake. (For 13×9-inch pan, double all glaze ingredients; simmer 10 to 12 minutes.)

PEANUT BUTTER FROSTING

Makes about 3½ cups

1 (8-ounce) package cream cheese, softened
1 (14-ounce) can Eagle® Brand Sweetened Condensed Milk (NOT evaporated milk)
1 cup peanut butter

In small mixer bowl, beat cheese until fluffy. Gradually beat in sweetened condensed milk, then peanut butter until smooth. Use to frost one (8- or 9-inch) two-layer cake *or* 4 dozen cupcakes *or* one (15×10-inch) sheet cake. Refrigerate leftovers.

WALNUT RUM RAISIN CHEESECAKE

CHOCOLATE COCONUT PECAN TORTE

Makes one 8- or 9-inch cake

1 (18¼- or 18½-ounce) package
　chocolate cake mix
1 (14-ounce) can Eagle® Brand
　Sweetened Condensed Milk
　(NOT evaporated milk)
3 egg yolks, beaten
½ cup margarine or butter
1 (3½-ounce) can flaked coconut
　(1⅓ cups)
1 cup chopped pecans
1 teaspoon vanilla extract
2 cups frozen non-dairy whipped
　topping, thawed, *or* 1 cup
　(½ pint) Borden® Whipping
　Cream, whipped
　Pecan halves, optional

Preheat oven to 350°. Prepare cake mix
as package directs. Pour batter into 3
well-greased and floured 8- or 9-inch
round layer cake pans. Bake 20 minutes
or until wooden pick inserted near
center comes out clean. Remove from
pans; cool thoroughly. Meanwhile, in
heavy saucepan, combine sweetened
condensed milk, egg yolks and
margarine. Over medium heat, cook
and stir until thickened and bubbly,
about 10 minutes. Stir in coconut,
pecans and vanilla. Cool 10 minutes.
With sharp knife, remove crust from top
of each cake layer to within ½ inch of
edge. Spread equal portions of coconut-
pecan mixture between layers and on
top to within ½ inch of edge. Frost side
and ½-inch rim on top of cake with
whipped topping. Garnish with pecan
halves if desired. Refrigerate leftovers.

BLACK FOREST TORTE

Makes one 9-inch cake

1 (18¼- or 18½-ounce) package
　chocolate cake mix
1 (6-ounce) package semi-sweet
　chocolate chips
1 (14-ounce) can Eagle® Brand
　Sweetened Condensed Milk
　(NOT evaporated milk)
1 (21-ounce) can cherry pie filling,
　drained and chilled, reserving
　¼ cup sauce
½ teaspoon almond extract

Preheat oven to 350°. Prepare and bake
cake mix as package directs for two 9-
inch round layers. Remove from pans;
cool thoroughly. In heavy saucepan,
over medium heat, melt chips with
sweetened condensed milk. Cook and
stir until thickened, about 10 minutes.
Cool 20 minutes. Meanwhile, combine
cherries, reserved sauce and extract.
Place 1 cake layer on serving plate, top
side up. With sharp knife, remove crust
from top of cake layer to within ½ inch
of edge; top with half the chocolate
mixture, then the cherries. Top with
second cake layer and remaining
chocolate mixture. Garnish as desired.

BLACK FOREST TORTE (TOP), CHOCOLATE
COCONUT PECAN TORTE (BOTTOM)

DELUXE PINEAPPLE CAKE

Makes one 13×9-inch cake

2 (8-ounce) cans juice-pack crushed pineapple, *well drained*, reserving juice
Water
1 (18¼- or 18½-ounce) package yellow cake mix
3 eggs
1 (14-ounce) can Eagle® Brand Sweetened Condensed Milk (NOT evaporated milk)
⅓ cup vegetable oil
1 (3-ounce) package cream cheese, softened
¼ cup frozen pineapple juice concentrate, thawed
Few drops yellow food coloring, optional

Preheat oven to 350°. To reserved pineapple juice, add enough water to make 1 cup. In large mixer bowl, combine cake mix, 1 cup pineapple liquid, eggs, *⅓ cup* sweetened condensed milk and oil. Beat on low speed until moistened, then beat on high speed 3 minutes. Stir in *1 can* drained pineapple. Pour into well-greased and floured 13×9-inch baking pan. Bake 35 to 40 minutes or until wooden pick inserted near center comes out clean. Cool. Meanwhile, in medium bowl, beat cheese until fluffy. Gradually beat in remaining sweetened condensed milk until smooth. Stir in juice concentrate, food coloring if desired, then remaining *1 can* drained pineapple. Chill. Spread evenly over cooled cake. Refrigerate leftovers.

DOUBLE LEMON CAKE

Makes one 13×9-inch cake

1 (18¼- or 18½-ounce) package lemon cake mix
1 (14-ounce) can Eagle® Brand Sweetened Condensed Milk (NOT evaporated milk)
2 egg yolks*
½ cup ReaLemon® Lemon Juice from Concentrate
1 teaspoon grated lemon rind, optional
Few drops yellow food coloring, optional
Whipped topping or whipped cream

Preheat oven to 350°. Prepare and bake cake mix as package directs for 13×9-inch cake. Meanwhile, in medium bowl, beat sweetened condensed milk and egg yolks. Stir in ReaLemon® brand, rind and food coloring if desired. Spread evenly over hot cake. Return to oven and bake 8 minutes longer. Cool. Chill. Serve with whipped topping. Garnish as desired. Refrigerate leftovers.

*Use Only Grade A clean, uncracked eggs.

EGG NOG CHEESECAKE

Makes one 9-inch cheesecake

1¼ cups vanilla wafer crumbs (about 36 wafers)
¼ cup sugar
¼ cup margarine or butter, melted
3 (8-ounce) packages cream cheese, softened
1 (14-ounce) can Eagle® Brand Sweetened Condensed Milk (NOT evaporated milk)
3 eggs
¼ cup dark rum
1 teaspoon vanilla extract
½ teaspoon ground nutmeg
    Rum Sauce

Preheat oven to 300°. Combine crumbs, sugar and margarine; press firmly on bottom of 9-inch springform pan *or* 13×9-inch baking pan. In large mixer bowl, beat cheese until fluffy. Gradually beat in sweetened condensed milk until smooth. Add eggs; mix well. Stir in rum, vanilla and nutmeg. Pour into prepared pan. Bake 40 to 50 minutes or until cake springs back when lightly touched. Cool. Chill. Serve with Rum Sauce. Refrigerate leftovers.

Rum Sauce: In small bowl, dissolve 1 tablespoon cornstarch in 1 cup water. In medium saucepan, melt 2 tablespoons margarine or butter. Stir in ⅓ cup firmly packed light brown sugar and cornstarch mixture. Bring to a boil, stirring constantly. Reduce heat; simmer 10 minutes. Remove from heat; add 2 tablespoons dark rum. Cool. Just before serving, stir in ½ cup chopped pecans. (Makes about 1¼ cups)

TROPICAL ORANGE CAKE

Makes one 13×9-inch cake

1 (18¼- or 18½-ounce) package white cake mix
1 cup water
2 eggs
1 (14-ounce) can Eagle® Brand Sweetened Condensed Milk (NOT evaporated milk)
2 teaspoons grated orange rind
1 (3½-ounce) can flaked coconut (1⅓ cups)
¼ cup frozen orange juice concentrate, thawed

Preheat oven to 350°. In large mixer bowl, combine cake mix, water, eggs, ⅓ *cup* sweetened condensed milk and rind. Beat on low speed until moistened, then beat on high speed 3 minutes. Stir in *1 cup* coconut. Pour into well-greased and floured 13×9-inch baking pan. Bake 30 minutes or until wooden pick inserted near center comes out clean. Meanwhile, in medium bowl, combine remaining sweetened condensed milk, remaining ⅓ *cup* coconut and juice concentrate. Spread evenly over cooled cake. Chill. Refrigerate leftovers.

TROPICAL ORANGE CAKE

APPLE SPICE CUSTARD CAKE

Makes 10 to 12 servings

1 (18¼-ounce) package spice cake mix
2 medium all-purpose apples, pared, cored and finely chopped (about 2 cups)
1 (14-ounce) can Eagle® Brand Sweetened Condensed Milk (NOT evaporated milk)
1 (8-ounce) container Borden® Sour Cream
¼ cup ReaLemon® Lemon Juice from Concentrate
Ground cinnamon

Preheat oven to 350°. Prepare cake mix as package directs; stir in apples. Pour into well-greased and floured 13×9-inch baking pan. Bake 30 minutes or until wooden pick inserted near center comes out clean. Meanwhile, in medium bowl, combine sweetened condensed milk, sour cream and ReaLemon® brand. Remove cake from oven; spread cream mixture over top. Return to oven; bake 10 minutes longer or until set. Sprinkle with cinnamon. Cool. Refrigerate leftovers.

RICH CARAMEL CAKE

Makes one 13×9-inch cake

1 (14-ounce) package caramels, unwrapped
½ cup margarine or butter
1 (14-ounce) can Eagle® Brand Sweetened Condensed Milk (NOT evaporated milk)
1 (18¼- or 18½-ounce) package chocolate cake mix
1 cup coarsely chopped pecans

Preheat oven to 350°. In heavy saucepan, over low heat, melt caramels and margarine. Remove from heat; add sweetened condensed milk. Mix well. Prepare cake mix as package directs. Spread *2 cups* batter into greased 13×9-inch baking pan; bake 15 minutes. Spread caramel mixture evenly over cake; spread remaining cake batter over caramel mixture. Top with nuts. Return to oven; bake 30 to 35 minutes or until cake springs back when lightly touched. Cool.

CHEESELESS "CHEESECAKE"

Makes 9 servings

4 eggs, separated
1 (14-ounce) can Eagle® Brand Sweetened Condensed Milk (NOT evaporated milk)
3 tablespoons ReaLemon® Lemon Juice from Concentrate
1½ teaspoons cornstarch
12 slices zwieback toast, crushed (about 1 cup)

Preheat oven to 350°. In medium bowl, beat egg yolks. Add sweetened condensed milk, ReaLemon® brand and cornstarch; mix well. In small mixer bowl, beat egg whites until stiff but not dry; fold into sweetened condensed milk mixture. Sprinkle half the zwieback crumbs into greased 9-inch square baking pan. Pour filling evenly over crumbs. Top with remaining crumbs. Bake 30 minutes or until wooden pick inserted near center comes out clean. Cool to room temperature. Chill. Cut into squares. Refrigerate leftovers.

NEW YORK STYLE CHEESECAKE

Makes one 9-inch cheesecake

1¼ cups graham cracker crumbs

¼ cup sugar

⅓ cup margarine or butter, melted

4 (8-ounce) packages cream cheese, softened

1 (14-ounce) can Eagle® Brand Sweetened Condensed Milk (NOT evaporated milk)

4 eggs

⅓ cup unsifted flour

1 tablespoon vanilla extract

½ teaspoon grated lemon rind

Preheat oven to 300°. Combine crumbs, sugar and margarine; press firmly on bottom of 9-inch springform pan. In large mixer bowl, beat cheese until fluffy. Gradually beat in sweetened condensed milk until smooth. Add eggs, flour, vanilla and rind; mix well. Pour into prepared pan. Bake 1 hour or until lightly browned. Cool. Chill. Garnish as desired. Refrigerate leftovers.

LEMON ANGEL ROLL

Makes 8 to 10 servings

1 (14½- or 16-ounce) package angel food cake mix
Confectioners' sugar
1 (14-ounce) can Eagle® Brand Sweetened Condensed Milk (NOT evaporated milk)
⅓ cup ReaLemon® Lemon Juice from Concentrate
2 teaspoons grated lemon rind
4 to 6 drops yellow food coloring, optional
1 (4-ounce) container frozen non-dairy whipped topping, thawed
½ cup flaked coconut, tinted yellow* if desired

Preheat oven to 350°. Line 15×10-inch jellyroll pan with aluminum foil, extending foil 1 inch over ends of pan. Prepare cake mix as package directs. Spread batter evenly into prepared pan. Bake 30 minutes or until top springs back when lightly touched. *Immediately* turn onto towel sprinkled with confectioners' sugar. Peel off foil; beginning at narrow end, roll up cake with towel, jellyroll-fashion. Cool thoroughly. Meanwhile, in medium bowl, combine sweetened condensed milk, ReaLemon® brand, rind and food coloring if desired; mix well. Fold in whipped topping. Unroll cake; trim edges. Spread with half the lemon filling; reroll. Place on serving plate, seam-side down; spread remaining filling over roll. Garnish with coconut. Chill. Store in refrigerator.

*To tint coconut: Combine coconut, ½ teaspoon water and 2 drops yellow food coloring in small plastic bag or bowl; shake or mix well.

Variations:

Chocolate Pecan Filling

½ cup margarine or butter
1 (1-ounce) square unsweetened
chocolate
1 (14-ounce) can Eagle® Brand
Sweetened Condensed Milk
(NOT evaporated milk)
1 (3½-ounce) can flaked coconut
(1⅓ cups)
¾ cup finely chopped pecans
1 teaspoon vanilla extract

Prepare cake roll as above. In medium saucepan, melt margarine and chocolate with sweetened condensed milk. Over medium heat, cook and stir until mixture thickens, about 10 minutes. Add coconut, nuts and vanilla. Spread all filling on cake; proceed as above. Sprinkle with confectioners' sugar. Store covered at room temperature or in refrigerator.

Cranberry Filling

1 cup fresh *or* dry-pack frozen
cranberries
½ cup sugar
¼ cup water
1 (3-ounce) package cream cheese,
softened
1 (14-ounce) can Eagle® Brand
Sweetened Condensed Milk
(NOT evaporated milk)
¼ cup ReaLemon® Lemon Juice from
Concentrate
Few drops red food coloring,
optional

Prepare cake roll as above. In small saucepan, combine cranberries, sugar and water. Bring to a boil; reduce heat and simmer uncovered 5 to 7 minutes. *Drain* cranberries; puree in blender. Cool. In small mixer bowl, beat cheese until fluffy. Gradually beat in sweetened condensed milk and ReaLemon® brand until smooth. Stir in cranberries and food coloring if desired. Chill 1 hour. Reserving 1½ cups mixture for outside, spread remaining filling on cake; proceed as above.

1. Invert cake *immediately* onto towel sprinkled with confectioners' sugar. Peel off foil. Roll up cake with towel; cool.

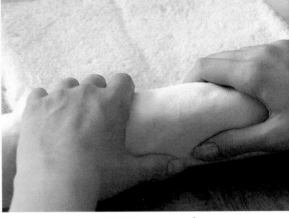

2. Unroll cooled cake. With serrated knife, trim uneven crust edges. Spread with filling.

3. Carefully roll cake and filling. Place on serving plate, seam-side down.

Cakes & Cheesecakes 71

CHOCOLATE PEAR UPSIDE-DOWN CAKE

Makes one 13×9-inch cake

1 (18¼- or 18½-ounce) package
    chocolate cake mix
1 (6-ounce) package semi-sweet
    chocolate chips
1 tablespoon margarine or butter
1 (14-ounce) can Eagle® Brand
    Sweetened Condensed Milk
    (NOT evaporated milk)
    Dash salt
½ teaspoon vanilla extract
2 tablespoons hot water
3 pears, pared, cored and sliced
⅔ cup finely chopped nuts

Preheat oven to 350°. Prepare cake mix
as package directs; set aside.
Meanwhile, in heavy saucepan, over
medium heat, melt chips and margarine
with sweetened condensed milk and
salt. Cook and stir until slightly
thickened, about 5 minutes. Remove
from heat; add vanilla and water.
Reserve *1 cup* chocolate mixture.
Arrange pears on bottom of greased
13×9-inch baking dish; sprinkle with
nuts. Drizzle with reserved *1 cup*
chocolate mixture. Pour cake batter over
chocolate. Bake 40 to 45 minutes or until
cake springs back when lightly touched.
Invert cake onto large serving tray; let
stand 5 minutes. Remove baking dish.
Cool. Serve with remaining chocolate
sauce. Refrigerate leftovers.

MICROWAVE: In 1-quart glass
measure, combine chips, margarine,
sweetened condensed milk and salt.
Cook on 100% power (high) 2½ to 3
minutes, stirring after each minute.
Proceed as above.

AMBROSIA COMPANY CAKE

Makes one 13×9-inch cake

1 (18¼- or 18½-ounce) package
    yellow or white cake mix
1 (14-ounce) can Eagle® Brand
    Sweetened Condensed Milk
    (NOT evaporated milk)
2 tablespoons frozen orange juice
    concentrate, thawed
1 teaspoon grated orange rind
1 (4-ounce) container frozen non-
    dairy whipped topping, thawed
⅓ cup flaked coconut, toasted
    Fresh orange slices, optional

Preheat oven to 350°. Prepare and bake
cake mix as package directs for 13×9-
inch cake. Cool. With table knife, poke
holes about 1 inch apart in cake halfway
to bottom. Combine sweetened
condensed milk, juice concentrate and
rind; spoon small amounts into each
hole in cake. Spread remaining mixture
evenly over top. Chill. Spread whipped
topping over cake; garnish with coconut
and orange slices if desired. Refrigerate
leftovers.

PEACH CREAM CAKE

Makes 10 to 12 servings

1 (10¾-ounce) prepared loaf angel food cake, frozen

1 (14-ounce) can Eagle® Brand Sweetened Condensed Milk (NOT evaporated milk)

1 cup cold water

1 teaspoon almond extract

1 (4-serving size) package *instant* vanilla flavor pudding mix

2 cups (1 pint) Borden® Whipping Cream, whipped

4 cups pared, sliced fresh peaches (about 2 pounds) *or* 1 (20-ounce) package frozen sliced peaches, thawed

Cut cake into ¼-inch slices; arrange half the slices on bottom of 13×9-inch baking dish. In large mixer bowl, combine sweetened condensed milk, water and extract. Add pudding mix; beat well. Chill 5 minutes. Fold in whipped cream. Spread half the cream mixture over cake slices; arrange half the peach slices on top. Repeat layering, ending with peach slices. Chill 4 hours or until set. Cut into squares to serve. Refrigerate leftovers.

Cakes & Cheesecakes 73

COCOA FUDGE CHEESECAKE

Makes one 9-inch cheesecake

Cocoa Crumb Crust
¼ cup margarine or butter, melted
½ cup unsweetened cocoa
3 (8-ounce) packages cream cheese, softened
1 (14-ounce) can Eagle® Brand Sweetened Condensed Milk (NOT evaporated milk)
4 eggs
1 tablespoon vanilla extract

Prepare Cocoa Crumb Crust; set aside. Preheat oven to 300°. Combine margarine and cocoa, stirring until smooth. In large mixer bowl, beat cheese until fluffy. Add cocoa mixture; mix well. Gradually beat in sweetened condensed milk until smooth. Add eggs and vanilla; mix well. Pour into prepared pan. Bake 1 hour and 5 minutes or until set (center will be soft). Cool. Chill. Garnish as desired. Refrigerate leftovers.

Cocoa Crumb Crust: In medium bowl, combine 1½ cups vanilla wafer crumbs (about 45 wafers), 6 tablespoons confectioners' sugar, ⅓ cup unsweetened cocoa and ⅓ cup margarine or butter, melted. Press firmly on bottom and ½ inch up side of 9-inch springform pan.

ORANGE CHEESECAKE ▶

Makes one 9-inch cheesecake

1½ cups vanilla wafer crumbs (about 36 wafers)
¼ cup margarine or butter, melted
3 (8-ounce) packages cream cheese, softened
1 (14-ounce) can Eagle® Brand Sweetened Condensed Milk (NOT evaporated milk)
¼ cup frozen orange juice concentrate, thawed
3 eggs
1 teaspoon grated orange rind
Fresh orange sections
Orange Glaze

Preheat oven to 300°. Combine crumbs and margarine; press firmly on bottom of 9-inch springform pan or 13×9-inch baking pan. In large mixer bowl, beat cheese until fluffy. Gradually beat in sweetened condensed milk until smooth. Add juice concentrate, eggs and rind; mix well. Pour into prepared pan. Bake 55 to 60 minutes or until set. Cool. Top with orange sections then Orange Glaze. Chill. Refrigerate leftovers.

Orange Glaze: In small saucepan, combine ¼ cup sugar and 2 teaspoons cornstarch. Add ½ cup orange juice and ¼ teaspoon grated orange rind; mix well. Over medium heat, cook and stir until thickened. Remove from heat; cool slightly. (For 13×9-inch pan, double all glaze ingredients.)

GERMAN CHOCOLATE CAKE

Makes one 13×9-inch cake

1 (18¼-ounce) package German chocolate cake mix
1 cup water
3 eggs plus 1 egg yolk
½ cup vegetable oil
1 (14-ounce) can Eagle® Brand Sweetened Condensed Milk (NOT evaporated milk)
3 tablespoons margarine or butter
⅓ cup chopped pecans
⅓ cup flaked coconut
1 teaspoon vanilla extract

Preheat oven to 350°. In large mixer bowl, combine cake mix, water, *3 eggs,* oil and *⅓ cup* sweetened condensed milk. Beat on low speed until moistened, then beat on high speed 2 minutes. Pour into well-greased and floured 13×9-inch baking pan. Bake 40 to 45 minutes or until wooden pick inserted near center comes out clean. In small saucepan, combine remaining sweetened condensed milk, egg yolk and margarine. Over medium heat, cook and stir until thickened, about 6 minutes. Add pecans, coconut and vanilla; spread over warm cake.

BOSTON CREAM PIE

Makes one 9-inch cake

1 (9-inch) prepared yellow cake layer, split
1 tablespoon cornstarch
¾ cup water
1 (14-ounce) can Eagle® Brand Sweetened Condensed Milk (NOT evaporated milk)
2 egg yolks
2½ teaspoons vanilla extract
⅛ teaspoon salt
1 (1-ounce) square unsweetened chocolate

In small saucepan, dissolve cornstarch in water; stir in ⅔ *cup* sweetened condensed milk, egg yolks, *2 teaspoons* vanilla and *dash* salt; mix well. Over medium heat, cook and stir until thickened, about 10 minutes. Remove from heat; cool 15 minutes. Chill 15 minutes. Meanwhile, in small saucepan, combine remaining sweetened condensed milk, chocolate and *dash* salt. Over medium heat, cook and stir until chocolate melts and mixture thickens, about 10 minutes. Remove from heat; stir in remaining ½ *teaspoon* vanilla. Place bottom half of cake on serving plate; spread with custard. Top with top half of cake; pour frosting in center of cake; spread to edge. Chill at least 2 hours before serving. Refrigerate leftovers.

ORANGE SPICE CAKE

Makes one 8- or 9-inch cake

1 (18½-ounce) package spice cake mix
1 (14-ounce) can Eagle® Brand Sweetened Condensed Milk (NOT evaporated milk)
1 (6-ounce) can frozen orange juice concentrate, thawed
2 teaspoons grated orange rind
1 (4-ounce) container frozen non-dairy whipped topping, thawed

Preheat oven to 350°. Prepare and bake cake mix as package directs for two 8- or 9-inch round layers. Remove from pans; cool. Split layers. In medium bowl, combine sweetened condensed milk, juice concentrate and rind; mix well. Fold in whipped topping. Chill at least 1 hour. Use about ⅔ cup orange mixture between each layer; use remainder to frost top and side. Chill. Refrigerate leftovers.

EASY CHOCO-APPLESAUCE CAKE

Makes one 15×10-inch cake

1 (15-ounce) jar applesauce
1 (14-ounce) can Eagle® Brand Sweetened Condensed Milk (NOT evaporated milk)
½ cup margarine or butter, melted
3 eggs
1 (1-ounce) square unsweetened chocolate, melted
2 teaspoons vanilla extract
2½ cups biscuit baking mix
½ teaspoon ground cinnamon
¾ cup chopped nuts
1 (16-ounce) can ready-to-spread chocolate frosting

Preheat oven to 325°. In large mixer bowl, beat applesauce, sweetened condensed milk, margarine, eggs, chocolate and vanilla. Add biscuit mix and cinnamon; mix well. Stir in nuts. Turn into lightly greased 15×10-inch jellyroll pan. Bake 25 to 30 minutes or until wooden pick inserted near center comes out clean. Cool. Frost with chocolate frosting.

MICROWAVE CHEESECAKE

Makes one 10-inch cheesecake

⅓ cup margarine or butter

1¼ cups graham cracker crumbs

¼ cup sugar

2 (8-ounce) packages cream cheese, softened

1 (14-ounce) can Eagle® Brand Sweetened Condensed Milk (NOT evaporated milk)

3 eggs

¼ cup ReaLemon® Lemon Juice from Concentrate

1 (8-ounce) container Borden® Sour Cream

In 10-inch microwave-safe quiche dish or pie plate, melt margarine loosely covered on 100% power (high) 1 minute. Add crumbs and sugar; press on bottom of dish. Cook on 100% power (high) 1½ minutes, rotating dish once. In 2-quart glass measure, beat cheese until fluffy. Beat in sweetened condensed milk until smooth. Add eggs, then ReaLemon® brand; mix well. Cook on 70% power (medium-high) 6 to 8 minutes or until hot, stirring every 2 minutes. Pour into dish. Cook on 50% power (medium) 6 to 8 minutes or until center is set, rotating dish once. Top with sour cream. Cool. Chill. Serve with fruit. Refrigerate leftovers.

FUDGE RIBBON CAKE

Makes one 10-inch cake

1 (18¼- or 18½-ounce) package
    chocolate cake mix
1 (8-ounce) package cream cheese,
    softened
2 tablespoons margarine or butter,
    softened
1 tablespoon cornstarch
1 (14-ounce) can Eagle® Brand
    Sweetened Condensed Milk
    (NOT evaporated milk)
1 egg
1 teaspoon vanilla extract
    Chocolate Glaze

Preheat oven to 350°. Prepare cake mix
as package directs. Pour batter into *well-
greased* and floured 10-inch bundt pan.
In small mixer bowl, beat cheese,
margarine and cornstarch until fluffy.
Gradually beat in sweetened condensed
milk, then egg and vanilla until smooth.
Pour evenly over cake batter. Bake 50 to
55 minutes or until wooden pick
inserted near center comes out clean.
Cool 10 minutes. Remove from pan.
Cool. Drizzle with Chocolate Glaze.
Refrigerate leftovers.

Chocolate Glaze: In small saucepan,
over low heat, melt 1 (1-ounce) square
unsweetened or semi-sweet chocolate
and 1 tablespoon margarine or butter
with 2 tablespoons water. Remove from
heat. Stir in ¾ cup confectioners' sugar
and ½ teaspoon vanilla extract. Stir
until smooth and well blended. (Makes
about ⅓ cup)

Fudge Ribbon Sheet Cake: Prepare
cake mix as package directs. Pour batter
into well-greased and floured 15×10-
inch jellyroll pan. Prepare cream cheese
topping as above; spoon evenly over
batter. Bake 20 minutes or until wooden
pick inserted near center comes out
clean. Cool. Frost with 1 (16-ounce) can
ready-to-spread chocolate frosting.

APPLE CINNAMON CHEESECAKE

Makes one 9-inch cheesecake

½ cup plus 1 tablespoon margarine or butter, softened
¼ cup firmly packed light brown sugar
1 cup unsifted flour
¼ cup quick-cooking oats
¼ cup finely chopped walnuts
½ teaspoon ground cinnamon
2 (8-ounce) packages cream cheese, softened
1 (14-ounce) can Eagle® Brand Sweetened Condensed Milk (NOT evaporated milk)
3 eggs
½ cup frozen apple juice concentrate, thawed
2 medium all-purpose apples, cored, pared and sliced (about 2 cups)
Cinnamon-Apple Glaze

Preheat oven to 300°. In small mixer bowl, beat ½ cup margarine and sugar until fluffy. Add flour, oats, nuts and cinnamon; mix well. Press firmly on bottom and halfway up side of 9-inch springform pan. Bake 10 minutes. Meanwhile, in large mixer bowl, beat cheese until fluffy. Gradually beat in sweetened condensed milk until smooth. Add eggs and juice concentrate; mix well. Pour into prepared crust. Bake 45 minutes or until cake springs back when lightly touched. Cool slightly. In large skillet, cook apples in remaining *1 tablespoon* margarine until tender-crisp. Arrange on top of cheesecake; drizzle with Cinnamon Apple Glaze. Chill. Refrigerate leftovers.

Cinnamon-Apple Glaze: In small saucepan, combine ¼ cup frozen apple juice concentrate, thawed, 1 teaspoon cornstarch and ¼ teaspoon ground cinnamon; mix well. Over low heat, cook and stir until thickened and clear. Add few drops red food coloring if desired. (Makes about ¼ cup)

NO-BAKE MINI CHEESECAKES

Makes 12 cheesecakes

1 (8-ounce) package cream cheese, softened
1 (14-ounce) can Eagle® Brand Sweetened Condensed Milk (NOT evaporated milk)
⅓ cup ReaLemon® Lemon Juice from Concentrate
½ cup Borden® Sour Cream
12 (3-inch) tart shells *or* 12 vanilla wafers placed in paper-lined muffin cups

In large mixer bowl, beat cheese until fluffy. Gradually beat in sweetened condensed milk until smooth. Stir in ReaLemon® brand and sour cream. Chill 20 minutes. Spoon into tart shells. Chill 2 hours or until set. Garnish as desired. Refrigerate leftovers.

Tip: To store in freezer, freeze 2 hours or until firm; cover and return to freezer. Thaw 45 minutes before serving. Garnish as desired.

BUTTERSCOTCH CHEESECAKE

Makes one 9-inch cheesecake

1½ cups graham cracker crumbs
⅓ cup firmly packed brown sugar
⅓ cup margarine or butter, melted
1 (14-ounce) can Eagle® Brand
    Sweetened Condensed Milk
    (NOT evaporated milk)
¾ cup cold water
1 (4-serving size) package
    butterscotch flavor pudding mix
3 (8-ounce) packages cream cheese,
    softened
3 eggs
1 teaspoon vanilla extract
    Whipped cream
    Crushed hard butterscotch candy

Preheat oven to 375°. Combine crumbs, sugar and margarine; press firmly on bottom of 9-inch springform pan. In medium saucepan, combine sweetened condensed milk and water; mix well. Stir in pudding mix. Over medium heat, cook and stir until thickened and bubbly. In large mixer bowl, beat cheese until fluffy. Beat in eggs and vanilla, then pudding mixture. Pour into prepared pan. Bake 50 minutes or until golden brown around edge (center will be soft). Cool to room temperature. Chill. Garnish with whipped cream and crushed candy. Refrigerate leftovers.

LEMON PARTY CHEESECAKE

Makes one 13×9-inch cheesecake

1 (18¼- or 18½-ounce) package
yellow cake mix*

4 eggs

¼ cup vegetable oil

2 (8-ounce) packages cream cheese,
softened

1 (14-ounce) can Eagle® Brand
Sweetened Condensed Milk
(NOT evaporated milk)

¼ to ⅓ cup ReaLemon® Lemon Juice
from Concentrate

2 teaspoons grated lemon rind,
optional

1 teaspoon vanilla extract

Preheat oven to 300°. Reserve ½ cup dry cake mix. In large mixer bowl, combine remaining cake mix, 1 egg and oil; mix well (mixture will be crumbly). Press firmly on bottom and halfway up sides of greased 13×9-inch baking dish. In same bowl, beat cheese until fluffy. Gradually beat in sweetened condensed milk until smooth. Add remaining 3 eggs and reserved ½ cup cake mix; on medium speed, beat 1 minute. Stir in remaining ingredients. Pour into prepared dish. Bake 50 to 55 minutes or until center is set. Cool to room temperature. Chill. Cut into squares. Garnish as desired. Refrigerate leftovers.

*If "pudding added" mix is used, decrease oil to 3 tablespoons.

PEANUT BUTTER CHEESECAKE

Makes one 9-inch cheesecake

1½ cups finely crushed creme-filled chocolate sandwich cookies (about 18 cookies)
2 tablespoons margarine or butter, melted
2 (8-ounce) packages cream cheese, softened
½ cup peanut butter
1 (14-ounce) can Eagle® Brand Sweetened Condensed Milk (NOT evaporated milk)
4 eggs
1 teaspoon vanilla extract

Preheat oven to 300°. Combine cookie crumbs and margarine; press firmly on bottom of 9-inch springform pan. In large mixer bowl, beat cheese and peanut butter until fluffy. Gradually beat in sweetened condensed milk until smooth. Add eggs and vanilla; mix well. Pour into prepared pan. Bake 50 to 55 minutes or until cake springs back when lightly touched. Cool to room temperature. Chill. Garnish as desired. Refrigerate leftovers.

CHOCOLATE WALNUT CAKE

Makes one 13×9-inch cake

1 (18¼- or 18½-ounce) package chocolate cake mix
1 cup coarsely chopped walnuts
1 (14-ounce) can Eagle® Brand Sweetened Condensed Milk (NOT evaporated milk)
2 (1-ounce) squares unsweetened chocolate
Dash salt
1 tablespoon water
½ teaspoon vanilla extract

Prepare cake mix as package directs, adding ½ cup nuts. Bake as package directs for 13×9-inch cake. Cool. In heavy saucepan, over low heat, combine sweetened condensed milk, chocolate and salt. Cook and stir until chocolate melts and mixture thickens, about 10 minutes. Remove from heat. Add water and vanilla; cool. Spread on cake. Garnish with remaining nuts.

MAGIC-QUICK CHOCOLATE FROSTING

Makes about 1½ cups

2 (1-ounce) squares unsweetened chocolate
1 (14-ounce) can Eagle® Brand Sweetened Condensed Milk (NOT evaporated milk)
Dash salt
1 tablespoon water
½ teaspoon vanilla extract

In heavy saucepan, over medium heat, melt chocolate with sweetened condensed milk and salt. Cook and stir until thickened, about 10 minutes. Remove from heat. Stir in water; cool. Stir in vanilla. Use to frost one (8- or 9-inch) two-layer cake or one (13×9-inch) cake. Store at room temperature.

MICROWAVE: In 1-quart glass measure, combine chocolate, sweetened condensed milk and salt. Cook on 100% power (high) 3 minutes, stirring after 1½ minutes. Stir until smooth. Proceed as above.

◀ MAPLE PUMPKIN CHEESECAKE

Makes one 9-inch cheesecake

1¼ cups graham cracker crumbs
¼ cup sugar
¼ cup margarine or butter, melted
3 (8-ounce) packages cream cheese, softened
1 (14-ounce) can Eagle® Brand Sweetened Condensed Milk (NOT evaporated milk)
1 (16-ounce) can pumpkin (2 cups)
3 eggs
1 (8-ounce) bottle Cary's® Pure Maple Syrup
1½ teaspoons ground cinnamon
1 teaspoon ground nutmeg
½ teaspoon salt
Maple Pecan Glaze

Preheat oven to 300°. Combine crumbs, sugar and margarine; press firmly on bottom of 9-inch springform pan *or* 13×9-inch baking pan. In large mixer bowl, beat cheese until fluffy. Gradually beat in sweetened condensed milk until smooth. Add pumpkin, eggs, *¼ cup* maple syrup, cinnamon, nutmeg and salt; mix well. Pour into prepared pan. Bake 1 hour and 15 minutes or until cake springs back when lightly touched (center will be slightly soft). Cool. Chill. Top with Maple Pecan Glaze. Refrigerate leftovers.

Maple Pecan Glaze: In saucepan, combine remaining *¾ cup* maple syrup and 1 cup (½ pint) Borden® Whipping Cream; bring to a boil. Boil rapidly 15 to 20 minutes; stir occasionally. Add ½ cup chopped pecans. (Makes about 1¼ cups)

CHERRY DUMPLIN' CAKE

Makes 6 to 8 servings

2 (16-ounce) cans red tart pitted cherries, well drained
1 (14-ounce) can Eagle® Brand Sweetened Condensed Milk (NOT evaporated milk)
1 teaspoon almond extract
¾ cup plus 2 tablespoons cold margarine or butter
2 cups biscuit baking mix
½ cup firmly packed brown sugar
½ cup chopped nuts

Preheat oven to 325°. In medium bowl, combine cherries, sweetened condensed milk and extract. In large bowl, cut *¾ cup* margarine into *1½ cups* biscuit mix until crumbly. Stir in cherry mixture. Spread in greased 9-inch square baking pan. In small bowl, combine remaining *½ cup* biscuit mix and sugar; cut in remaining *2 tablespoons* margarine until crumbly. Stir in nuts. Sprinkle evenly over cherry mixture. Bake 1 hour and 10 minutes or until golden brown. Serve warm with ice cream if desired. Refrigerate leftovers.

MICROWAVE: In 2-quart round baking dish, prepare as above. Cook on 100% power (high) 16 to 18 minutes.

GERMAN CHOCOLATE CHEESECAKE SQUARES

Makes one 15×10-inch cheesecake

1½ cups graham cracker crumbs
½ cup sugar
½ cup margarine or butter, melted
3 (8-ounce) packages cream cheese, softened
1 (14-ounce) can Eagle® Brand Sweetened Condensed Milk (NOT evaporated milk)
2 (4-ounce) packages sweet cooking chocolate, melted
3 eggs
1 tablespoon vanilla extract
Coconut Pecan Topping

Preheat oven to 350°. Combine crumbs, sugar and margarine; press on bottom of 15×10-inch jellyroll pan. In large mixer bowl, beat cheese until fluffy. Gradually beat in sweetened condensed milk until smooth. Add remaining ingredients except topping; mix well. Pour into prepared pan. Bake 20 minutes or until center is set. Cool. Top with Coconut Pecan Topping. Chill. Refrigerate leftovers.

Coconut Pecan Topping: In heavy saucepan, combine 1 (14-ounce) can Eagle® Brand Sweetened Condensed Milk (NOT evaporated milk) and 3 egg yolks; mix well. Add ½ cup margarine or butter. Over medium-low heat, cook and stir until thickened and bubbly, 8 to 10 minutes. Remove from heat; stir in 1 (3½-ounce) can flaked coconut (1⅓ cups), 1 cup chopped pecans and 1 teaspoon vanilla. Cool 10 minutes. (Makes about 2¾ cups)

DOUBLE LEMON CHEESECAKE

Makes one 9-inch cheesecake

1¼ cups graham cracker crumbs
¼ cup sugar
⅓ cup margarine or butter, melted
4 (8-ounce) packages cream cheese, softened
1 (14-ounce) can Eagle® Brand Sweetened Condensed Milk (NOT evaporated milk)
4 eggs
2 tablespoons flour
¼ cup ReaLemon® Lemon Juice from Concentrate
Lemon Glaze

Preheat oven to 350°. Combine crumbs, sugar and margarine; press firmly on bottom of 9-inch springform pan. In large mixer bowl, beat cheese until fluffy. Gradually beat in sweetened condensed milk until smooth. Add eggs and flour; mix well. Stir in ReaLemon® brand. Pour into prepared pan. Bake 1 hour or until lightly browned. Cool. Top with Lemon Glaze. Chill. Serve with fresh strawberries if desired. Refrigerate leftovers.

Lemon Glaze: In small saucepan, combine ⅓ cup sugar, 1 tablespoon cornstarch and dash salt. Add ⅓ cup water, ¼ cup ReaLemon® brand and 1 egg yolk; mix well. Over medium heat, cook and stir until thickened and bubbly. Remove from heat; add 1 tablespoon margarine or butter. Stir until well blended. Cool slightly. (Makes about ¾ cup)

DOUBLE CHERRY CAKE

Makes one 13×9-inch cake

1 (18½-ounce) package cherry flavor cake mix
1 (8-ounce) package cream cheese, softened
1 (14-ounce) can Eagle® Brand Sweetened Condensed Milk (NOT evaporated milk)
⅓ cup ReaLemon® Lemon Juice from Concentrate
1 teaspoon almond extract
1 (21-ounce) can cherry pie filling, chilled

Preheat oven to 350°. Prepare and bake cake as package directs for 13×9-inch cake. Cool. Meanwhile, in large mixer bowl, beat cheese until fluffy. Gradually beat in sweetened condensed milk until smooth. Stir in ReaLemon® brand and ½ *teaspoon* almond extract. Spread evenly over cooled cake. Chill at least 3 hours. Just before serving, stir remaining ½ *teaspoon* almond extract into pie filling; spread on cake. Refrigerate leftovers.

COOKIES &
COOKIE BARS

Clockwise from top right:
Choco-Coconut Layer Bars,
Peanut Blossoms and Easy
Peanut Butter Cookies
(recipes, page 90)

CHOCO-COCONUT LAYER BARS

Makes 24 bars

⅓ cup margarine or butter, melted
¾ cup unsifted flour
½ cup sugar
2 tablespoons unsweetened cocoa
1 egg
1 (14-ounce) can Eagle® Brand Sweetened Condensed Milk (NOT evaporated milk)
1 (3½-ounce) can flaked coconut (1⅓ cups)
Flavor Variations*
1 (6-ounce) package semi-sweet chocolate chips

Preheat oven to 350° (325° for glass dish). In medium bowl, combine margarine, flour, sugar, cocoa and egg; mix well. Spread evenly into lightly greased 9-inch square baking pan. In small bowl, combine ¾ cup sweetened condensed milk, coconut and desired flavor variation; spread over chocolate layer. Bake 20 minutes or until lightly browned around edges. In heavy saucepan, over low heat, melt chips with remaining sweetened condensed milk. Remove from heat; spread evenly over coconut layer. Cool. Chill. Cut into bars. Store loosely covered at room temperature.

*Flavor Variations:

Almond: Add 1 cup chopped slivered almonds and ½ teaspoon almond extract.

Mint: Add ½ teaspoon peppermint extract and 4 drops green food coloring if desired.

Cherry: Add 2 (6-ounce) jars maraschino cherries, chopped and well drained on paper towels.

EASY PEANUT BUTTER COOKIES

Makes about 5 dozen

1 (14-ounce) can Eagle® Brand Sweetened Condensed Milk (NOT evaporated milk)
¾ to 1 cup peanut butter
1 egg
1 teaspoon vanilla extract
2 cups biscuit baking mix
Granulated sugar

Preheat oven to 350°. In large mixer bowl, beat sweetened condensed milk, peanut butter, egg and vanilla until smooth. Add biscuit mix; mix well. Chill at least 1 hour. Shape into 1-inch balls. Roll in sugar. Place 2 inches apart on ungreased baking sheets. Flatten with fork. Bake 6 to 8 minutes or until *lightly browned (do not overbake)*. Cool. Store tightly covered at room temperature.

Peanut Blossoms: Shape as above; *do not flatten.* Bake as above. Press solid milk chocolate candy drop in center of each ball immediately after baking.

Peanut Butter & Jelly Gems: Press thumb in center of each ball of dough; fill with jelly, jam or preserves. Bake as above.

Any-Way-You-Like'em Cookies: Stir *1 cup* semi-sweet chocolate chips *or* chopped peanuts *or* raisins *or* flaked coconut into dough. Proceed as above.

COCONUT MACAROONS

Makes about 4 dozen

2 (7-ounce) packages *flaked* coconut (5⅓ cups)
1 (14-ounce) can Eagle® Brand Sweetened Condensed Milk (NOT evaporated milk)
2 teaspoons vanilla extract
1½ teaspoons almond extract

Preheat oven to 350°. In large bowl, combine coconut, sweetened condensed milk and extracts; mix well. Drop by rounded teaspoonfuls onto aluminum-foil-lined and *generously greased* baking sheets; garnish as desired. Bake 8 to 10 minutes or until lightly browned around edges. *Immediately* remove from baking sheets (macaroons will stick if allowed to cool). Store loosely covered at room temperature.

Chocolate: Omit almond extract. Add 4 (1-ounce) squares unsweetened chocolate, melted. Proceed as above.

Chocolate Chip: Omit almond extract. Add 1 cup mini chocolate chips. Proceed as above.

Cherry Nut: Omit almond extract. Add 1 cup chopped nuts and 2 tablespoons maraschino cherry syrup. Press maraschino cherry half into center of each macaroon before baking.

Rum Raisin: Omit almond extract. Add 1 cup raisins and 1 teaspoon rum flavoring. Proceed as above.

Almond Brickle: Add ½ cup almond brickle chips. Proceed as above. Bake 10 to 12 minutes. Cool 3 minutes; remove from baking sheets.

Maple Walnut: Omit almond extract. Add ½ cup finely chopped walnuts and ½ teaspoon maple flavoring. Proceed as above.

Nutty Oat: Omit almond extract. Add 1 cup oats and 1 cup chopped nuts. Proceed as above.

Tip: To reduce cost, omit 1 (7-ounce) package coconut and substitute 2 cups fresh bread crumbs (4 slices bread).

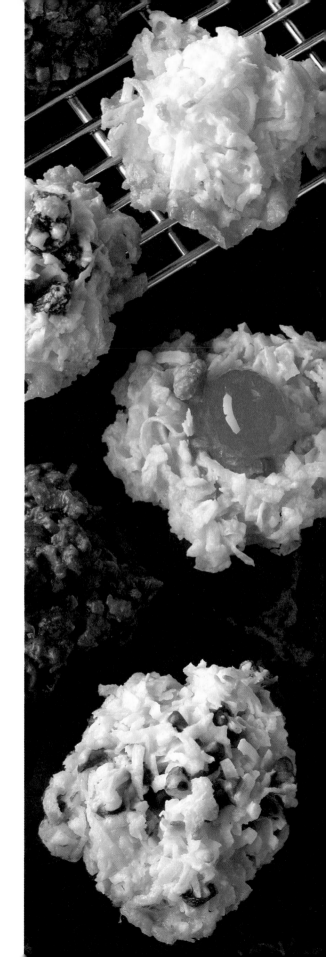

PUMPKIN CHEESECAKE BARS

Makes 48 bars

1 (16-ounce) package pound cake mix
3 eggs
2 tablespoons margarine or butter, melted
4 teaspoons pumpkin pie spice
1 (8-ounce) package cream cheese, softened
1 (14-ounce) can Eagle® Brand Sweetened Condensed Milk (NOT evaporated milk)
1 (16-ounce) can pumpkin (2 cups)
½ teaspoon salt
1 cup chopped nuts

Preheat oven to 350°. In large mixer bowl, combine cake mix, *1 egg*, margarine and *2 teaspoons* pumpkin pie spice; beat on low speed until crumbly. Press on bottom of 15×10-inch jellyroll pan. In same mixer bowl, beat cheese until fluffy. Gradually beat in sweetened condensed milk until smooth. Add remaining *2 eggs*, pumpkin, remaining *2 teaspoons* pumpkin pie spice and salt; mix well. Pour over crust; sprinkle with nuts. Bake 30 to 35 minutes or until set. Cool. Chill. Cut into bars. Store covered in refrigerator.

WALNUT-OAT TOPPED COOKIE BARS

Makes 48 bars

2 cups unsifted flour
¾ cup sugar
½ cup margarine or butter, melted
2 eggs
1½ cups coarsely chopped walnuts
1 (14-ounce) can Eagle® Brand Sweetened Condensed Milk (NOT evaporated milk)
1 cup quick-cooking oats
1½ teaspoons vanilla extract
1 (6-ounce) package semi-sweet chocolate chips

Preheat oven to 350°. In small mixer bowl, combine flour, sugar, margarine and eggs; beat until smooth. Spread into lightly greased 13×9-inch baking pan. In medium bowl, stir together *1 cup* walnuts, sweetened condensed milk, oats and vanilla. Spread evenly over cookie base. Top with chips and remaining *½ cup* walnuts; press down firmly. Bake 30 to 35 minutes or until golden brown. Cool. Chill. Cut into bars. Store loosely covered at room temperature.

PUMPKIN CHEESECAKE BARS

APPLE NUT BARS

Makes 48 bars

3 cups finely chopped all-purpose
    apples (4 medium)
1 (16.1-ounce) package nut bread mix
1 (14-ounce) can Eagle® Brand
    Sweetened Condensed Milk
    (NOT evaporated milk)
1 cup chopped nuts
3 eggs
2 teaspoons vanilla extract
1½ teaspoons ground cinnamon
½ teaspoon ground nutmeg
    Cream Cheese Frosting

Preheat oven to 350°. In large bowl,
combine all ingredients except frosting;
mix well. Pour into greased and floured
15×10-inch jellyroll pan. Bake 30
minutes or until golden. Cool. Spread
with frosting. Cut into bars. Garnish as
desired. Store covered at room
temperature.

Cream Cheese Frosting: In small mixer
bowl, beat 2 (3-ounce) packages cream
cheese, softened, ½ cup margarine or
butter, softened, and 1 teaspoon vanilla
until fluffy. Add 4 cups sifted
confectioners' sugar; mix well. (Makes
about 2½ cups)

CHOCO-DIPPED PEANUT BUTTER COOKIES

Makes about 5 dozen

1 (14-ounce) can Eagle® Brand
    Sweetened Condensed Milk
    (NOT evaporated milk)
¾ to 1 cup peanut butter
1 egg
1 teaspoon vanilla extract
2 cups biscuit baking mix
1 pound chocolate confectioners'
    coating,* melted

Preheat oven to 350°. In large mixer
bowl, beat sweetened condensed milk,
peanut butter, egg and vanilla until
smooth. Add biscuit mix; mix well. Chill
at least 1 hour. Shape into 1-inch balls.
Place 2 inches apart on ungreased
baking sheets. Bake 10 to 12 minutes or
until lightly browned around edges (*do
not overbake*). Cool. Partially dip cookies
into melted confectioners' coating. Place
on waxed paper-lined baking sheets. Let
stand until firm. Store tightly covered at
room temperature.

*Confectioners' coating can be
purchased in candy specialty stores.

BUTTERSCOTCH CHEESECAKE BARS

Makes 36 bars

1 (12-ounce) package butterscotch-
    flavored chips
⅓ cup margarine or butter
2 cups graham cracker crumbs
1 cup chopped nuts
1 (8-ounce) package cream cheese,
    softened
1 (14-ounce) can Eagle® Brand
    Sweetened Condensed Milk
    (NOT evaporated milk)
1 egg
1 teaspoon vanilla extract

Preheat oven to 350° (325° for glass
dish). In medium saucepan, over low
heat, melt chips and margarine; stir in
crumbs and nuts. Press half the mixture
firmly on bottom of greased 13×9-inch
baking pan. In large mixer bowl, beat
cheese until fluffy. Gradually beat in
sweetened condensed milk then egg and
vanilla until smooth. Pour into prepared
pan; top evenly with remaining crumb
mixture. Bake 25 to 30 minutes or until
wooden pick inserted near center comes
out clean. Cool. Chill. Cut into bars.
Store covered in refrigerator.

CHEESECAKE TOPPED BROWNIES

Makes 40 brownies

1 (21½-ounce) package fudge brownie mix
1 (8-ounce) package cream cheese, softened
2 tablespoons margarine or butter, softened
1 tablespoon cornstarch
1 (14-ounce) can Eagle® Brand Sweetened Condensed Milk (NOT evaporated milk)
1 egg
1 teaspoon vanilla extract
  Ready-to-spread chocolate frosting, optional

Preheat oven to 350°. Prepare brownie mix as package directs. Spread into well-greased 13×9-inch baking pan. In small mixer bowl, beat cheese, margarine and cornstarch until fluffy. Gradually beat in sweetened condensed milk, then egg and vanilla until smooth. Pour evenly over brownie batter. Bake 45 minutes or until top is lightly browned. Cool. Spread with frosting if desired. Cut into bars. Store covered in refrigerator.

TINY LEMON RAISIN TARTS

Makes about 4 dozen

1 cup margarine or butter, softened
2 (3-ounce) packages cream cheese, softened
2 cups unsifted flour
1 (14-ounce) can Eagle® Brand Sweetened Condensed Milk (NOT evaporated milk)
1 egg
2 tablespoons ReaLemon® Lemon Juice from Concentrate
1 tablespoon grated lemon rind
1¼ cups raisins
   Confectioners' sugar, optional

In large mixer bowl, beat margarine and cheese until fluffy; stir in flour. Cover; chill 1 hour. Divide dough into quarters. On floured surface, shape 1 quarter into a ball. Divide into 12 balls. Place each ball in a 1¾-inch muffin cup; press on bottom and up side of each cup. Repeat with remaining dough. In small mixer bowl, beat sweetened condensed milk, egg and ReaLemon® brand until smooth; stir in rind. Divide raisins evenly among prepared muffin cups; fill with sweetened condensed milk mixture. Bake in preheated 375° oven 20 minutes or until lightly browned. Cool in pans; remove. Sprinkle with confectioners' sugar if desired. Store tightly covered at room temperature.

CHOCOLATE ALMOND BROWNIES

Makes 16 brownies

1¼ cups unsifted flour
2 tablespoons sugar
½ cup cold margarine or butter
1 cup chopped almonds, toasted
1 (14-ounce) can Eagle® Brand Sweetened Condensed Milk (NOT evaporated milk)
¼ cup unsweetened cocoa
1 egg
2 tablespoons amaretto liqueur or 1 teaspoon almond extract
½ teaspoon baking powder
6 (1¼-ounce) white candy bars with almonds, broken into small pieces

Preheat oven to 350°. In medium bowl, combine *1 cup* flour and sugar; cut in margarine until crumbly. Add *¼ cup* almonds. Press on bottom of 9-inch round or square baking pan. Bake 15 minutes. In large mixer bowl, beat sweetened condensed milk, remaining *¼ cup* flour, cocoa, egg, amaretto and baking powder until smooth. Stir in candy pieces and *½ cup* almonds. Spread over prepared crust. Top with remaining *¼ cup* almonds. Bake 30 minutes or until center is set. Cool. Cut into wedges.

MAGIC COOKIE BARS ▲

Makes 24 to 36 bars

½ cup margarine or butter
1½ cups graham cracker *or* other
    crumbs*
1 (14-ounce) can Eagle® Brand
    Sweetened Condensed Milk
    (NOT evaporated milk)
1 cup semi-sweet chocolate chips *or*
    other toppings**
1 (3½-ounce) can flaked coconut
    (1⅓ cups)
1 cup chopped nuts***

Preheat oven to 350° (325° for glass
dish). In 13×9-inch baking pan, melt
margarine in oven. Sprinkle crumbs
over margarine; pour sweetened
condensed milk evenly over crumbs.
Top with chips then coconut and nuts;
press down firmly. Bake 25 to 30
minutes or until lightly browned. Cool.
Chill if desired. Cut into bars. Store
loosely covered at room temperature.

*Crumbs

Vanilla wafer	Quick-cooking
Chocolate wafer	oats
Gingersnap cookie	Wheat germ

**Toppings

Peanut butter flavored chips
Butterscotch-flavored chips
Mint chocolate chips
Plain multi-colored candy-coated
   chocolate pieces
Raisins
Chopped dried apricots
Almond brickle chips
Banana chips
Chopped candied cherries
Small gumdrop candies
Miniature marshmallows

***Nuts

Walnuts	Peanuts
Pecans	Cashews
Almonds	Macadamia nuts

Flavor Variations:

Mint: Combine ½ teaspoon peppermint extract and 4 drops green food coloring if desired with sweetened condensed milk. Proceed as above.

Mocha: Add 1 tablespoon instant coffee and 1 tablespoon chocolate-flavored syrup with sweetened condensed milk. Proceed as above.

Peanut Butter: Beat ⅓ cup peanut butter with sweetened condensed milk. Proceed as above.

Maple: Combine ½ to 1 teaspoon maple flavoring with sweetened condensed milk. Proceed as above.

BANANA COOKIE BARS

Makes 24 to 36 bars

½ cup margarine or butter
1½ cups graham cracker crumbs
1 (14-ounce) can Eagle® Brand
    Sweetened Condensed Milk
    (NOT evaporated milk)
2 medium bananas, mashed (about
    1 cup)
1 (6-ounce) package semi-sweet
    chocolate chips
1 (3½-ounce) can flaked coconut
    (1⅓ cups)
1 cup chopped nuts

Preheat oven to 350° (325° for glass dish). In 13×9-inch baking pan, melt margarine in oven. Sprinkle crumbs over margarine. In small bowl, combine sweetened condensed milk and bananas; pour evenly over crumbs. Top with remaining ingredients; press down firmly. Bake 25 to 30 minutes or until lightly browned. Cool. Chill. Cut into bars. Store covered in refrigerator.

MACAROON ALMOND CRUMB BARS

Makes 36 bars

1 (18¼- or 18½-ounce) package
    chocolate cake mix
¼ cup vegetable oil
2 eggs
1 (14-ounce) can Eagle® Brand
    Sweetened Condensed Milk
    (NOT evaporated milk)
½ to 1 teaspoon almond extract
1½ cups coconut macaroon crumbs
    (about 8 macaroons)
1 cup chopped slivered almonds

Preheat oven to 350° (325° for glass dish). In large mixer bowl, combine cake mix, oil and *1 egg*; beat on medium speed until crumbly. Press firmly on bottom of greased 13×9-inch baking pan. In medium bowl, combine sweetened condensed milk, remaining egg and extract; mix well. Add *1 cup* macaroon crumbs and almonds. Spread evenly over crust. Sprinkle with remaining *½ cup* crumbs. Bake 30 to 35 minutes or until lightly browned. Cool. Cut into bars. Store loosely covered at room temperature.

DOUBLE CHOCOLATE FANTASY BARS

Makes 36 bars

1 (18¼- or 18½-ounce) package
    chocolate cake mix
¼ cup vegetable oil
1 egg
1 cup chopped nuts
1 (14-ounce) can Eagle® Brand
    Sweetened Condensed Milk
    (NOT evaporated milk)
1 (6-ounce) package semi-sweet
    chocolate chips
1 teaspoon vanilla extract
    Dash salt

Preheat oven to 350°. In large mixer bowl, combine cake mix, oil and egg; beat on medium speed until crumbly. Stir in nuts. Reserving 1½ cups crumb mixture, press remainder firmly on bottom of greased 13×9-inch baking pan. In small saucepan, combine remaining ingredients. Over medium heat, cook and stir until chips melt. Pour over prepared crust. Top with reserved crumb mixture. Bake 25 to 30 minutes or until bubbly. Cool. Cut into bars. Store loosely covered at room temperature.

MILK CHOCOLATE BROWNIES

Makes 40 brownies

1 (12-ounce) package semi-sweet
    chocolate chips
¼ cup margarine or butter
2 cups biscuit baking mix
1 (14-ounce) can Eagle® Brand
    Sweetened Condensed Milk
    (NOT evaporated milk)
1 egg, beaten
1 teaspoon vanilla extract
1 cup chopped walnuts
    Confectioners' sugar

Preheat oven to 350°. In large saucepan, over low heat, melt *1 cup* chips with margarine; remove from heat. Add biscuit mix, sweetened condensed milk, egg and vanilla. Stir in nuts and remaining chips. Turn into well-greased 13×9-inch baking pan. Bake 20 to 25 minutes or until brownies begin to pull away from sides of pan. Cool. Sprinkle with confectioners' sugar. Cut into squares. Store tightly covered at room temperature.

TOP TO BOTTOM: DOUBLE CHOCOLATE FANTASY BARS, MACAROON ALMOND CRUMB BARS, TOFFEE BARS (PAGE 100)

GERMAN CHOCOLATE SNACKIN' BARS ▲

Makes 36 bars

1 (4-ounce) package sweet cooking
 chocolate
¼ cup margarine or butter
1 (14-ounce) can Eagle® Brand
 Sweetened Condensed Milk
 (NOT evaporated milk)
2 eggs
½ cup biscuit baking mix
1 teaspoon vanilla extract
1 (7-ounce) package flaked coconut
 (2⅔ cups)
1 cup chopped pecans

Preheat oven to 350° (325° for glass
dish). In medium saucepan, over low
heat, melt chocolate with margarine.
Remove from heat; stir in *½ cup*
sweetened condensed milk, eggs, biscuit
mix and vanilla. Spread evenly into
greased 13×9-inch baking pan. In
medium bowl, combine remaining
sweetened condensed milk and coconut.
Spoon in small amounts evenly over
chocolate mixture. Sprinkle with nuts;
press down firmly. Bake 25 minutes or
until wooden pick inserted near center
comes out clean. Cool. Cut into bars.
Store loosely covered at room
temperature.

TOFFEE BARS

Makes 36 bars

½ cup margarine or butter, melted
1 cup oats
½ cup firmly packed brown sugar
½ cup unsifted flour
½ cup finely chopped walnuts
¼ teaspoon baking soda
1 (14-ounce) can Eagle® Brand
 Sweetened Condensed Milk
 (NOT evaporated milk)
2 teaspoons vanilla extract
1 (6-ounce) package semi-sweet
 chocolate chips

Preheat oven to 350°. Combine
6 tablespoons margarine, oats, sugar,
flour, nuts and baking soda. Press firmly
on bottom of greased 13×9-inch baking
pan; bake 10 to 15 minutes or until
lightly browned. Meanwhile, in medium
saucepan, combine remaining
2 tablespoons margarine and sweetened
condensed milk. Over medium heat,
cook and stir until mixture thickens
slightly, about 15 minutes. Remove from
heat; stir in vanilla. Pour over crust.
Return to oven; bake 10 to 15 minutes
longer or until golden brown. Remove
from oven; *immediately* sprinkle chips on
top. Let stand 1 minute; spread while
still warm. Cool. Cut into bars. Store
tightly covered at room temperature.

CHOCOLATE MINT CHEESECAKE BARS

Makes 24 to 36 bars

1¼ cups unsifted flour
1 cup confectioners' sugar
½ cup unsweetened cocoa
¼ teaspoon baking soda
1 cup cold margarine or butter
1 (8-ounce) package cream cheese, softened
1 (14-ounce) can Eagle® Brand Sweetened Condensed Milk (NOT evaporated milk)
2 eggs
1½ teaspoons peppermint extract
2 to 3 drops green or red food coloring, optional
Chocolate Glaze

Preheat oven to 350°. In large bowl, combine flour, sugar, cocoa and baking soda; cut in margarine until crumbly (mixture will be dry). Press firmly on bottom of 13×9-inch baking pan. Bake 15 minutes. Meanwhile, in large mixer bowl, beat cheese until fluffy. Gradually beat in sweetened condensed milk until smooth. Add eggs, extract and food coloring if desired; mix well. Pour over prepared crust. Bake 20 minutes or until lightly browned around edges. Cool. Spread or drizzle with Chocolate Glaze. Chill. Cut into bars. Store covered in refrigerator.

Chocolate Glaze: Combine 1 cup confectioners' sugar, 2 tablespoons unsweetened cocoa, 1 tablespoon margarine or butter, melted, and 2 tablespoons hot water; mix well. Immediately spread or drizzle on bars. (Makes about ½ cup)

MAKE-AHEAD S'MORES

Makes 32 servings

8 (1-ounce) squares semi-sweet chocolate
1 (14-ounce) can Eagle® Brand Sweetened Condensed Milk (NOT evaporated milk)
1 teaspoon vanilla extract
32 (4¾×2⅛-inch) whole graham crackers
2 cups Campfire® Miniature Marshmallows

In heavy saucepan, over low heat, melt chocolate. Add sweetened condensed milk and vanilla; cook and stir until smooth. Making 1 sandwich at a time, spread 1 tablespoon chocolate mixture on each of 2 whole graham crackers; sprinkle one with marshmallows and gently press second graham cracker chocolate-side down on top. Repeat with remaining ingredients. Carefully break each sandwich in half. Wrap in plastic wrap; store at room temperature.

MICROWAVE: In 1-quart glass measure, combine chocolate, sweetened condensed milk and vanilla. Cook on 100% power (high) 2½ minutes. Stir until smooth. Proceed as above.

MAKE-AHEAD S'MORES

PETITE MACAROON CUPS

Makes about 4 dozen

1 cup margarine or butter, softened
2 (3-ounce) packages cream cheese, softened
2 cups unsifted flour
1 (14-ounce) can Eagle® Brand Sweetened Condensed Milk (NOT evaporated milk)
2 eggs, beaten
1½ teaspoons vanilla extract
½ teaspoon almond extract
1 (3½-ounce) can flaked coconut (1⅓ cups)

In large mixer bowl, beat margarine and cheese until fluffy; stir in flour. Cover; chill 1 hour. Divide dough into quarters. On floured surface, shape 1 quarter into a smooth ball. Divide into 12 balls. Place each ball in a 1¾-inch muffin cup; press evenly on bottom and up side of each cup. Repeat with remaining dough. In medium bowl, combine sweetened condensed milk, eggs and extracts; mix well. Stir in coconut. Fill muffin cups ¾ full. Bake in preheated 375° oven 16 to 18 minutes or until lightly browned. Cool in pans; remove. Store loosely covered at room temperature.

Chocolate Macaroon Cups: Beat ¼ cup unsweetened cocoa into egg mixture; proceed as above.

PETITE MACAROON CUPS (LEFT), CHUNKY BROWNIES WITH A CRUST (RIGHT)

CHUNKY BROWNIES WITH A CRUST

Makes 36 brownies

1¼ cups unsifted flour
¼ cup sugar
½ cup cold margarine or butter
1 (14-ounce) can Eagle® Brand
    Sweetened Condensed Milk
    (NOT evaporated milk)
¼ cup unsweetened cocoa
1 egg
1 teaspoon vanilla extract
½ teaspoon baking powder
1 (8-ounce) bar milk chocolate candy,
    broken into small pieces
¾ cup chopped nuts
    Confectioners' sugar, optional

Preheat oven to 350°. In medium bowl, combine *1 cup* flour and sugar; cut in margarine until crumbly. Press on bottom of 13×9-inch baking pan. Bake 15 minutes. In large mixer bowl, beat sweetened condensed milk, cocoa, egg, remaining *¼ cup* flour, vanilla and baking powder. Stir in chocolate pieces and nuts. Spread over prepared crust. Bake 20 minutes or until center is set. Cool. Sprinkle with confectioners' sugar if desired. Store loosely covered at room temperature.

MACAROON KISSES

Makes about 3½ dozen

2 (7-ounce) packages *flaked* coconut
    (5⅓ cups)
1 (14-ounce) can Eagle® Brand
    Sweetened Condensed Milk
    (NOT evaporated milk)
2 teaspoons vanilla extract
1½ teaspoons almond extract
42 solid milk chocolate candy drops,
    unwrapped

Preheat oven to 350°. In large bowl, combine coconut, sweetened condensed milk and extracts; mix well. Drop by heaping teaspoonfuls onto aluminum foil-lined and *generously greased* baking sheets. Bake 8 to 10 minutes or until lightly browned around edges. Press a candy drop in center of each macaroon. Immediately remove from baking sheets (macaroons will stick if allowed to cool). Cool thoroughly or chill until candy drops are set. Store loosely covered at room temperature.

CHOCOLATE PECAN BARS

Makes 36 bars

1¼ cups unsifted flour
1 cup confectioners' sugar
½ cup unsweetened cocoa
1 cup cold margarine or butter
1 (14-ounce) can Eagle® Brand
    Sweetened Condensed Milk
    (NOT evaporated milk)
1 egg
2 teaspoons vanilla extract
1½ cups chopped pecans

Preheat oven to 350° (325° for glass dish). In large bowl, combine flour, sugar and cocoa; cut in margarine until crumbly. Press firmly on bottom of 13×9-inch baking pan. Bake 15 minutes. Meanwhile, in medium bowl, beat sweetened condensed milk, egg and vanilla. Stir in pecans. Spread evenly over crust. Bake 25 minutes or until lightly browned. Cool. Cut into bars. Store covered in refrigerator.

APPLESAUCE FRUITCAKE BARS

Makes 48 bars

1 (14-ounce) can Eagle® Brand
   Sweetened Condensed Milk
   (NOT evaporated milk)
2 eggs
¼ cup margarine or butter, melted
2 teaspoons vanilla extract
3 cups biscuit baking mix
1 (15-ounce) jar applesauce
1 cup chopped dates
1 (6-ounce) container green candied
   cherries, chopped
1 (6-ounce) container red candied
   cherries, chopped
1 cup chopped nuts
1 cup raisins
   Confectioners' sugar

Preheat oven to 325°. In large mixer bowl, beat sweetened condensed milk, eggs, margarine and vanilla. Stir in remaining ingredients except confectioners' sugar; mix well. Spread evenly into well-greased and floured 15×10-inch jellyroll pan. Bake 35 to 40 minutes or until wooden pick inserted in center comes out clean. Cool. Sprinkle with confectioners' sugar. Cut into bars. Store tightly covered at room temperature.

CHOCOLATE PEANUT BUTTER CHIP COOKIES ▶

Makes about 4 dozen

8 (1-ounce) squares semi-sweet
    chocolate
3 tablespoons margarine or butter
1 (14-ounce) can Eagle® Brand
    Sweetened Condensed Milk
    (NOT evaporated milk)
2 cups biscuit baking mix
1 egg
1 teaspoon vanilla extract
1 cup peanut butter flavored chips

Preheat oven to 350°. In large saucepan,
over low heat, melt chocolate and
margarine with sweetened condensed
milk; remove from heat. Add biscuit
mix, egg and vanilla; with mixer, beat
until smooth. Cool to room
temperature. Stir in chips. Shape into
1¼-inch balls. Place 2 inches apart on
ungreased baking sheets. Bake 6 to 8
minutes or until tops are slightly
crusted (*do not overbake*). Cool. Store
tightly covered at room temperature.

NO-BAKE PEANUTTY CHOCOLATE DROPS

Makes about 5 dozen

½ cup margarine or butter
⅓ cup unsweetened cocoa
1 (14-ounce) can Eagle® Brand
    Sweetened Condensed Milk
    (NOT evaporated milk)
2½ cups quick-cooking oats
1 cup chopped peanuts
½ cup peanut butter

In medium saucepan, over medium
heat, melt margarine; stir in cocoa.
Bring mixture to a boil. Remove from
heat; stir in remaining ingredients. Drop
by teaspoonfuls onto waxed paper-lined
baking sheets; chill 2 hours or until set.
Store loosely covered in refrigerator.

TWO-TONE CHEESECAKE BARS

Makes 24 to 36 bars

2 cups finely crushed creme-filled
    chocolate sandwich cookies
    (about 24 cookies)
3 tablespoons margarine or butter,
    melted
3 (8-ounce) packages cream cheese,
    softened
1 (14-ounce) can Eagle® Brand
    Sweetened Condensed Milk
    (NOT evaporated milk)
3 eggs
2 teaspoons vanilla extract
2 (1-ounce) squares unsweetened
    chocolate, melted
    Chocolate Glaze

Preheat oven to 300°. Combine crumbs
and margarine; press firmly on bottom
of 13×9-inch baking pan. In large mixer
bowl, beat cheese until fluffy. Gradually
beat in sweetened condensed milk until
smooth. Add eggs and vanilla; mix well.
Pour half the batter evenly over
prepared crust. Stir melted chocolate
into remaining batter; pour evenly over
yellow batter. Bake 55 to 60 minutes or
until set. Cool. Top with Chocolate
Glaze. Chill. Cut into bars. Refrigerate
leftovers.

Chocolate Glaze: In small saucepan,
over low heat, melt 2 (1-ounce) squares
unsweetened chocolate with 2
tablespoons margarine or butter and a
dash salt. Remove from heat; add 1¾
cups confectioners' sugar and 3
tablespoons hot water; mix well.
Immediately spread over bars. (Makes
about 1 cup)

PEANUT BUTTER BRICKLE BARS

Makes 48 bars

2 cups quick-cooking oats
1½ cups unsifted flour
1 cup chopped dry-roasted peanuts
1 cup firmly packed brown sugar
1 teaspoon baking soda
½ teaspoon salt
1 cup margarine or butter, melted
1 (14-ounce) can Eagle® Brand
    Sweetened Condensed Milk
    (NOT evaporated milk)
½ cup peanut butter
1 (6-ounce) package almond brickle
    chips

Preheat oven to 375°. In large bowl,
combine oats, flour, peanuts, sugar,
baking soda and salt; stir in margarine
until crumbly. Reserving 1½ cups crumb
mixture, press remainder on bottom of
greased 15×10-inch jellyroll pan. Bake
12 minutes. Meanwhile, in small mixer
bowl, beat sweetened condensed milk
with peanut butter until smooth; spread
evenly over prepared crust to within ¼
inch of edge. In medium bowl, combine
reserved crumb mixture and brickle
chips. Sprinkle evenly over peanut
butter mixture; press down firmly. Bake
20 minutes or until golden brown. Cool.
Cut into bars. Store loosely covered at
room temperature.

PUMPKIN PECAN PIE BARS

Makes 48 bars

½ cup margarine or butter, softened
1 cup firmly packed brown sugar
1½ cups unsifted flour
1 cup oats
1 teaspoon baking powder
1 teaspoon salt
1 (16-ounce) can pumpkin (2 cups)
1 (14-ounce) can Eagle® Brand
    Sweetened Condensed Milk
    (NOT evaporated milk)
2 eggs, beaten
2 teaspoons pumpkin pie spice
1½ teaspoons vanilla extract
1 cup chopped pecans
    Confectioners' sugar, optional

Preheat oven to 350°. In large mixer bowl, beat margarine and sugar until fluffy; add flour, oats, baking powder and ½ *teaspoon* salt. Mix until crumbly. Reserving ½ *cup* crumb mixture, press remainder on bottom of 15×10-inch jellyroll pan. Bake 20 minutes. Meanwhile, in medium bowl, combine pumpkin, sweetened condensed milk, eggs, pumpkin pie spice, vanilla and remaining ½ *teaspoon* salt. Spread over crust. In small bowl, combine reserved crumb mixture with pecans; sprinkle over pumpkin mixture. Bake 30 to 35 minutes or until set. Cool. Sprinkle with confectioners' sugar if desired. Cut into bars. Store covered in refrigerator.

CASHEW PEANUT BUTTER BARS

Makes 36 bars

1 cup unsifted flour
¼ cup firmly packed brown sugar
½ teaspoon baking powder
¼ teaspoon baking soda
½ cup cold margarine or butter
1 tablespoon vanilla extract
3 cups Campfire® Miniature Marshmallows
1 (14-ounce) can Eagle® Brand Sweetened Condensed Milk (NOT evaporated milk)
1 cup peanut butter flavored chips *or* ½ cup creamy peanut butter
1 (3-ounce) can chow mein noodles
1 cup coarsely chopped cashews *or* peanuts

Preheat oven to 350°. In medium bowl, combine flour, sugar, baking powder and baking soda; cut in margarine and *1 teaspoon* vanilla until crumbly. Press firmly on bottom of ungreased 13×9-inch baking pan. Bake 15 minutes or until lightly browned. Top evenly with marshmallows; bake 2 minutes longer or until marshmallows begin to puff. Remove from oven; cool. Meanwhile, in heavy saucepan, over medium heat, combine sweetened condensed milk and peanut butter chips; cook and stir until slightly thickened, 6 to 8 minutes. Remove from heat; stir in noodles, nuts and remaining *2 teaspoons* vanilla. Spread evenly over marshmallows. Cool. Chill. Cut into bars. Store loosely covered at room temperature.

DOUBLE CHOCOLATE CHERRY COOKIES

Makes about 10 dozen

1¼ cups margarine or butter, softened
1¾ cups sugar
2 eggs
1 tablespoon vanilla extract
3½ cups unsifted flour
¾ cup unsweetened cocoa
½ teaspoon baking powder
½ teaspoon baking soda
¼ teaspoon salt
2 (6-ounce) jars maraschino cherries, well drained and halved (about 60 cherries)
1 (6-ounce) package semi-sweet chocolate chips
1 (14-ounce) can Eagle® Brand Sweetened Condensed Milk (NOT evaporated milk)

Preheat oven to 350°. In large mixer bowl, beat margarine and sugar until fluffy; add eggs and vanilla. Mix well. Combine dry ingredients; stir into margarine mixture (dough will be stiff). Shape into 1-inch balls. Place 1 inch apart on ungreased baking sheets. Press cherry half into center of each cookie. Bake 8 to 10 minutes. Cool. In heavy saucepan, over medium heat, melt chips with sweetened condensed milk; cook until mixture thickens, about 3 minutes. Frost each cookie, covering cherry. Store loosely covered at room temperature.

Double Chocolate Pecan Cookies: Prepare cookies as above, omitting cherries. Flatten. Bake and frost as directed. Garnish each cookie with a pecan half.

PECAN PIE BARS

Makes 36 bars

2 cups unsifted flour
½ cup confectioners' sugar
1 cup cold margarine or butter
1 (14-ounce) can Eagle® Brand Sweetened Condensed Milk (NOT evaporated milk)
1 egg
1 teaspoon vanilla extract
1 (6-ounce) package almond brickle chips
1 cup chopped pecans

Preheat oven to 350° (325° for glass dish). In medium bowl, combine flour and sugar; cut in margarine until crumbly. Press firmly on bottom of 13×9-inch baking pan. Bake 15 minutes. Meanwhile, in medium bowl, beat sweetened condensed milk, egg and vanilla. Stir in chips and pecans. Spread evenly over crust. Bake 25 minutes or until golden brown. Cool. Cut into bars. Store covered in refrigerator.

TRIPLE LAYER COOKIE BARS

Makes 24 to 36 bars

½ cup margarine or butter
1½ cups graham cracker crumbs
1 (7-ounce) package flaked coconut (2⅔ cups)
1 (14-ounce) can Eagle® Brand Sweetened Condensed Milk (NOT evaporated milk)
1 (12-ounce) package semi-sweet chocolate chips
½ cup creamy peanut butter

Preheat oven to 350° (325° for glass dish). In 13×9-inch baking pan, melt margarine in oven. Sprinkle crumbs evenly over margarine. Top evenly with coconut then sweetened condensed milk. Bake 25 minutes or until lightly browned. In small saucepan, over low heat, melt chips with peanut butter. Spread evenly over hot coconut layer. Cool 30 minutes. Chill. Cut into bars. Store loosely covered at room temperature.

MINI FRUITCAKE MORSELS

Makes about 7 dozen

½ cup unsifted flour
1 teaspoon baking soda
1 jar None Such® Ready-to-Use Mincemeat (Regular *or* Brandy & Rum)
1 (14-ounce) can Eagle® Brand Sweetened Condensed Milk (NOT evaporated milk)
2 cups graham cracker crumbs
1 cup chopped nuts
3 eggs, beaten
Red and green candied cherries, halved

Preheat oven to 300°. In large bowl, combine flour and baking soda. Add remaining ingredients except cherries; mix well. Line 1¾-inch muffin cups with foil or paper liners or grease lightly. Spoon 1 level measuring tablespoon batter into each cup. Top each with cherry half. Bake 25 to 30 minutes or until wooden pick inserted near center comes out clean. Cool. Store loosely covered at room temperature.

CRUNCH BARS

Makes 36 bars

5 cups bite-size crispy rice or wheat squares
½ cup margarine or butter
1 cup butterscotch *or* peanut butter flavored chips
1 (3½-ounce) can flaked coconut (1⅓ cups)
1 (14-ounce) can Eagle® Brand Sweetened Condensed Milk (NOT evaporated milk)
1 cup chopped pecans

Preheat oven to 350° (325° for glass dish). Coarsely crush 3 *cups* cereal. In 13×9-inch baking pan, melt margarine in oven. Sprinkle crushed cereal over margarine; top evenly with chips, coconut, sweetened condensed milk, nuts and 2 *cups* uncrushed cereal. Press down firmly. Bake 25 to 30 minutes or until lightly browned. Cool. Cut into bars. Store loosely covered at room temperature.

FUDGY COOKIE WEDGE (BOTTOM LEFT),
CHOCOLATE STREUSEL BAR (TOP RIGHT)

FUDGY COOKIE WEDGES

Makes 36 wedges

1 (20-ounce) package refrigerated
cookie dough, any flavor
1 (12-ounce) package semi-sweet
chocolate chips
2 tablespoons margarine or butter
1 (14-ounce) can Eagle® Brand
Sweetened Condensed Milk
(NOT evaporated milk)
1 teaspoon vanilla extract
Chopped nuts

Preheat oven to 350°. Divide cookie
dough into thirds. With floured hands,
press on bottom of three aluminum foil-
lined 9-inch round cake pans *or* press
into 9-inch circles on ungreased baking
sheets. Bake 10 to 12 minutes or until
golden. Cool. In heavy saucepan, over
medium heat, melt chips and margarine
with sweetened condensed milk and
vanilla. Cook and stir until thickened,
about 5 minutes. Spread over cookie
circles. Top with nuts. Chill. Cut into
wedges. Store loosely covered at room
temperature.

MICROWAVE: Bake cookie dough as
above. In 1-quart glass measure,
combine remaining ingredients except
nuts. Cook on 100% power (high) 4
minutes, stirring after each minute.
Proceed as above.

CHOCOLATE STREUSEL BARS

Makes 24 to 36 bars

1¾ cups unsifted flour
1½ cups confectioners' sugar
½ cup unsweetened cocoa
1 cup cold margarine or butter
1 (8-ounce) package cream cheese, softened
1 (14-ounce) can Eagle® Brand Sweetened Condensed Milk (NOT evaporated milk)
1 egg
2 teaspoons vanilla extract
½ cup chopped nuts

Preheat oven to 350°. In large bowl, combine flour, sugar and cocoa. Cut in margarine until crumbly (mixture will be dry). Reserving 2 cups crumb mixture, press remainder firmly on bottom of 13×9-inch baking pan. Bake 15 minutes. In large mixer bowl, beat cheese until fluffy. Gradually beat in sweetened condensed milk until smooth. Add egg and vanilla; mix well. Pour over prepared crust. Combine nuts with reserved crumb mixture; sprinkle over cheese mixture. Bake 25 minutes or until bubbly. Cool. Chill. Cut into bars. Store covered in refrigerator.

CHOCOLATE 'N' OAT BARS

Makes 36 bars

1 cup unsifted flour
1 cup quick-cooking oats
¾ cup firmly packed light brown sugar
½ cup margarine or butter, softened
1 (14-ounce) can Eagle® Brand Sweetened Condensed Milk (NOT evaporated milk)
1 cup chopped nuts
1 (6-ounce) package semi-sweet chocolate chips

Preheat oven to 350° (325° for glass dish). In large bowl, combine flour, oats, sugar and margarine; mix well. Reserving ½ *cup* oat mixture, press remainder on bottom of 13×9-inch baking pan. Bake 10 minutes. Pour sweetened condensed milk evenly over crust. Sprinkle with nuts and chocolate chips. Top with reserved oat mixture; press down firmly. Bake 25 to 30 minutes or until lightly browned. Cool. Cut into bars. Store covered at room temperature.

CHOCOLATE 'N' OAT BARS

QUICK NO-BAKE BROWNIES

Makes 24 brownies

1 cup finely chopped nuts
2 (1-ounce) squares unsweetened chocolate
1 (14-ounce) can Eagle® Brand Sweetened Condensed Milk (NOT evaporated milk)
2½ cups vanilla wafer crumbs (about 60 wafers)

In buttered 9-inch square pan, sprinkle ¼ *cup* nuts. In heavy saucepan, over low heat, melt chocolate with sweetened condensed milk. Cook and stir until mixture thickens, about 10 minutes. Remove from heat; stir in crumbs and ½ *cup* nuts. Spread evenly into prepared pan. Top with remaining ¼ *cup* nuts. Chill 4 hours or until firm. Cut into squares. Store loosely covered at room temperature.

PEANUTTY OAT BARS

Makes 36 bars

¼ cup margarine or butter
1½ cups quick-cooking oats
1 (3½-ounce) can flaked coconut (1⅓ cups)
1 (14-ounce) can Eagle® Brand Sweetened Condensed Milk (NOT evaporated milk)
1 cup peanut butter flavored chips
1 cup chopped nuts

Preheat oven to 350° (325° for glass dish). In 13×9-inch baking pan, melt margarine in oven. Sprinkle oats over margarine, then coconut. Pour sweetened condensed milk evenly over top. Top evenly with chips then nuts; press down firmly. Bake 25 to 30 minutes or until lightly browned. Cool. Cut into bars. Store loosely covered at room temperature.

VERSATILE CUT-OUT COOKIES ▶

Makes about 6½ dozen

3⅓ cups unsifted flour
1 tablespoon baking powder
½ teaspoon salt
1 (14-ounce) can Eagle® Brand Sweetened Condensed Milk (NOT evaporated milk)
¾ cup margarine or butter, softened
2 eggs
2 teaspoons vanilla *or* 1½ teaspoons almond *or* lemon extract
Ready-to-spread frosting

Combine flour, baking powder and salt; set aside. In large bowl, beat sweetened condensed milk, margarine, eggs and vanilla until well blended. Add dry ingredients; mix well. Chill 2 hours. On floured surface, lightly knead dough to form a smooth ball. Divide into thirds. On well-floured surface, roll out each portion to ⅛-inch thickness. Cut with floured cookie cutter. Place 1 inch apart on greased baking sheets. Bake in preheated 350° oven 7 to 9 minutes or until lightly browned around edges. Cool. Frost and decorate as desired. Store loosely covered at room temperature.

Sandwich Cookies: Use 2½-inch cookie cutter. Bake as directed. Sandwich 2 cookies together with ready-to-spread frosting. Sprinkle with confectioners' sugar if desired. (Makes about 3 dozen)

PEANUT BUTTER SNACKIN' BARS

Makes 36 bars

1 (14-ounce) can Eagle® Brand
  Sweetened Condensed Milk
  (NOT evaporated milk)
1 cup peanut butter
1 egg
¼ cup water
1½ teaspoons vanilla extract
1½ cups biscuit baking mix
1 (6-ounce) package semi-sweet
  chocolate chips
½ cup chopped peanuts

Preheat oven to 350°. In large mixer
bowl, beat sweetened condensed milk,
peanut butter, egg, water and vanilla
until smooth. Add biscuit mix; mix well.
Stir in chips. Spread evenly in greased
13×9-inch baking pan. Sprinkle with
peanuts. Bake 30 to 35 minutes or until
wooden pick inserted near center comes
out clean. Cool. Cut into bars. Store
tightly covered at room temperature.

ALMOND TOFFEE BARS

Makes 24 to 36 bars

1½ cups unsifted flour
½ cup confectioners' sugar
¾ cup cold margarine or butter
1 (14-ounce) can Eagle® Brand
  Sweetened Condensed Milk
  (NOT evaporated milk)
1 egg
1 teaspoon almond extract
1 (7.12-ounce) package milk-
  chocolate-covered English toffee
  candy bars, cut into small pieces
  (6 bars)
1 cup chopped almonds

Preheat oven to 350° (325° for glass
dish). In medium bowl, combine flour
and sugar; cut in margarine until
crumbly. Press firmly on bottom of
13×9-inch baking pan. Bake 15 minutes.
Meanwhile, in large mixer bowl, beat
sweetened condensed milk, egg and
extract. Stir in toffee pieces and
almonds. Spread evenly over crust. Bake
20 minutes or until golden brown. Cool.
Cut into bars. Store covered in
refrigerator.

BUCKEYE COOKIE BARS

Makes 24 to 36 bars

1 (18¼- or 18½-ounce) package
  chocolate cake mix
¼ cup vegetable oil
1 egg
1 cup chopped peanuts
1 (14-ounce) can Eagle® Brand
  Sweetened Condensed Milk
  (NOT evaporated milk)
½ cup peanut butter

Preheat oven to 350° (325° for glass
dish). In large mixer bowl, combine cake
mix, oil and egg; beat on medium speed
until crumbly. Stir in peanuts. Reserving
1½ cups crumb mixture, press
remainder firmly on bottom of greased
13×9-inch baking pan. In medium bowl,
beat sweetened condensed milk with
peanut butter until smooth; spread over
prepared crust. Sprinkle with reserved
crumb mixture. Bake 25 to 30 minutes or
until set. Cool. Cut into bars. Store
loosely covered at room temperature.

DOUBLE CHOCOLATE COOKIES (LEFT),
BUCKEYE COOKIE BAR (RIGHT)

DOUBLE CHOCOLATE COOKIES

Makes about 4½ dozen

2 cups biscuit baking mix
1 (14-ounce) can Eagle® Brand Sweetened Condensed Milk (NOT evaporated milk)
8 (1-ounce) squares semi-sweet chocolate *or* 1 (12-ounce) package semi-sweet chocolate chips, melted
3 tablespoons margarine or butter, melted
1 egg
1 teaspoon vanilla extract
6 (1¼-ounce) white candy bars with almonds, broken into small pieces
¾ cup chopped nuts

Preheat oven to 350°. In large mixer bowl, combine all ingredients except candy pieces and nuts; beat until smooth. Stir in remaining ingredients. Drop by rounded teaspoonfuls, 2 inches apart, onto ungreased baking sheets. Bake 10 minutes or until tops are slightly crusted (*do not overbake*). Cool. Store tightly covered at room temperature.

Mint Chocolate: Omit white candy bars. Stir in ¾ cup mint-flavored chocolate chips. Proceed as above.

CHOCOLATE MINT BARS

Makes 48 bars

1 (6-ounce) package semi-sweet chocolate chips
1 (14-ounce) can Eagle® Brand Sweetened Condensed Milk (NOT evaporated milk)
¾ cup plus 2 tablespoons margarine or butter
½ teaspoon peppermint extract
1¼ cups firmly packed light brown sugar
1 egg
1½ cups unsifted flour
1½ cups quick-cooking oats
¾ cup chopped nuts
⅓ cup crushed hard peppermint candy, optional

Preheat oven to 350°. In heavy saucepan, over low heat, melt chips with sweetened condensed milk and *2 tablespoons* margarine; remove from heat. Add extract; set aside. In large mixer bowl, beat remaining *¾ cup* margarine and sugar until fluffy; beat in egg. Add flour and oats; mix well. With floured hands, press two-thirds oat mixture on bottom of greased 15×10-inch jellyroll pan; spread evenly with chocolate mixture. Add nuts to remaining oat mixture; crumble evenly over chocolate. Sprinkle with peppermint candy if desired. Bake 15 to 18 minutes or until edges are lightly browned. Cool. Cut into bars. Store loosely covered at room temperature.

TOP TO BOTTOM: DOUBLE PEANUT-CHOCO BARS, CHOCOLATE MINT BARS, LAYERED LEMON CRUMB BARS

DOUBLE PEANUT-CHOCO BARS

Makes 36 bars

1 (18¼- or 18½-ounce) package white cake mix
½ cup plus ⅓ cup peanut butter
1 egg
1 (14-ounce) can Eagle® Brand Sweetened Condensed Milk (NOT evaporated milk)
1 (6-ounce) package semi-sweet chocolate chips
¾ cup Spanish peanuts

Preheat oven to 350° (325° for glass dish). In large mixer bowl, combine cake mix, ½ *cup* peanut butter and egg; beat on low speed until crumbly. Press firmly on bottom of greased 13×9-inch baking pan. In medium bowl, combine sweetened condensed milk and remaining ⅓ *cup* peanut butter; mix well. Spread evenly over prepared crust. Top with chips and peanuts. Bake 30 to 35 minutes or until lightly browned. Cool. Cut into bars. Store loosely covered at room temperature.

LAYERED LEMON CRUMB BARS

Makes 36 bars

1 (14-ounce) can Eagle® Brand Sweetened Condensed Milk (NOT evaporated milk)
½ cup ReaLemon® Lemon Juice from Concentrate
1 teaspoon grated lemon rind
⅔ cup margarine or butter, softened
1 cup firmly packed light brown sugar
1½ cups unsifted flour
1 cup oats
1 teaspoon baking powder
½ teaspoon salt
½ teaspoon ground cinnamon
½ teaspoon ground nutmeg

Preheat oven to 350° (325° for glass dish). In small bowl, combine sweetened condensed milk, ReaLemon® brand and rind; set aside. In large mixer bowl, beat margarine and sugar until fluffy; add flour, oats, baking powder and salt. Mix until crumbly. Press half the oat mixture on bottom of lightly greased 13×9-inch baking pan. Top with lemon mixture. Stir spices into remaining crumb mixture; sprinkle evenly over lemon layer. Bake 20 to 25 minutes or until lightly browned. Cool. Chill. Cut into bars. Store covered in refrigerator.

QUICK FRUIT SNACK MUNCHIES

Makes about 5 dozen

1 (14-ounce) can Eagle® Brand Sweetened Condensed Milk (NOT evaporated milk)
2 cups finely chopped dried apricots or dates
¾ cup finely chopped nuts
1 teaspoon vanilla extract
1 (12-ounce) package butter- or cheese-flavored crackers

In heavy saucepan, over medium heat, combine sweetened condensed milk and apricots; cook and stir until thickened, about 8 minutes. Remove from heat; stir in nuts and vanilla. Spoon about 1 teaspoon mixture on cracker; top with another cracker. Repeat. Store loosely covered at room temperature.

MICROWAVE: In 1-quart glass measure, combine sweetened condensed milk and apricots. Cook on 50% power (medium) 5 to 6 minutes, stirring after 3 ·minutes. Stir in nuts and vanilla. Proceed as above.

GRANOLA BARS ▲

Makes 48 bars

3 cups oats
1 cup peanuts
1 cup raisins
1 cup sunflower meats
1½ teaspoons ground cinnamon
1 (14-ounce) can Eagle® Brand
   Sweetened Condensed Milk
   (NOT evaporated milk)
½ cup margarine or butter, melted

Preheat oven to 325°. Line 15×10-inch
jellyroll pan with aluminum foil; grease.
In large bowl, combine all ingredients;
mix well. Press evenly into prepared
pan. Bake 25 to 30 minutes or until
golden brown. Cool slightly; remove
from pan and peel off foil. Cut into
bars. Store loosely covered at room
temperature.

CHOCOLATE & FRUIT CHEESECAKE BARS

Makes 48 bars

1 (12-ounce) package semi-sweet
   chocolate chips
½ cup margarine or butter
2 cups graham cracker crumbs
1 cup chopped nuts
1 (8-ounce) package cream cheese,
   softened
1 (14-ounce) can Eagle® Brand
   Sweetened Condensed Milk
   (NOT evaporated milk)
1 egg
1 teaspoon vanilla extract
1 (9-ounce) package None Such®
   Condensed Mincemeat, crumbled

Preheat oven to 350°. In large saucepan, over low heat, melt chips and margarine; stir in crumbs and nuts. Press half the mixture firmly on bottom of greased 15×10-inch jellyroll pan (layer will be thin). In large mixer bowl, beat cheese until fluffy; gradually beat in sweetened condensed milk then egg and vanilla. Add mincemeat; mix well. Pour into prepared pan; top with remaining crumb mixture. Bake 25 to 30 minutes or until wooden pick inserted near center comes out clean. Cool to room temperature. Chill. Cut into bars. Store covered in refrigerator.

Butterscotch Variation: Substitute 1 (12-ounce) package butterscotch-flavored chips for chocolate chips. Proceed as directed.

CHOCOLATE ALMOND BARS

Makes 24 bars

1¼ cups graham cracker crumbs
 1 cup slivered almonds, toasted and chopped
 1 (14-ounce) can Eagle® Brand Sweetened Condensed Milk (NOT evaporated milk)
 ¼ cup margarine or butter, melted
 ½ teaspoon almond extract
 ½ teaspoon ground cinnamon, optional
 1 (6-ounce) package semi-sweet chocolate chips

Preheat oven to 350°. In large bowl, combine all ingredients except ½ cup chocolate chips; mix well. Spread evenly into greased 12×7-inch baking dish. Bake 20 minutes or until golden brown. Remove from oven; *immediately* sprinkle remaining ½ cup chips over top. Let stand 1 minute; spread while still warm. Cool. Cut into bars. Store loosely covered at room temperature.

MAGIC PEANUT COOKIE BARS

Makes 24 to 36 bars

½ cup margarine or butter
1½ cups graham cracker crumbs
 1 (14-ounce) can Eagle® Brand Sweetened Condensed Milk (NOT evaporated milk)
 2 cups (about ¾ pound) chocolate-covered peanuts
 1 (3½-ounce) can flaked coconut (1⅓ cups)

Preheat oven to 350° (325° for glass dish). In 13×9-inch baking pan, melt margarine in oven. Sprinkle crumbs over margarine; pour sweetened condensed milk evenly over crumbs. Top evenly with peanuts, then coconut; press down firmly. Bake 25 to 30 minutes or until lightly browned. Cool. Chill if desired. Cut into bars. Store loosely covered at room temperature.

MAGIC PEANUT COOKIE BARS

Strawberries & Cream Dessert
(recipe, page 124)

CLASSIC DESSERTS

STRAWBERRIES & CREAM DESSERT

Makes 10 to 12 servings

1 (14-ounce) can Eagle® Brand
    Sweetened Condensed Milk
    (NOT evaporated milk)
1½ cups cold water
1 (4-serving size) package *instant*
    vanilla flavor pudding mix
2 cups (1 pint) Borden® Whipping
    Cream, whipped
1 (10¾- *or* 12-ounce) prepared loaf
    pound cake, cut into cubes (about
    6 cups)
1 quart fresh strawberries, hulled
    and sliced
½ cup strawberry preserves
    Additional fresh strawberries
    Toasted slivered almonds

In large bowl, combine sweetened
condensed milk and water. Add
pudding mix; beat well. Chill 5 minutes.
Fold in whipped cream. Spoon *2 cups*
pudding mixture into 4-quart glass
serving bowl; top with half *each* of the
cake cubes, strawberries, preserves and
remaining pudding. Repeat layering,
ending with pudding. Garnish with
additional strawberries and almonds.
Chill. Refrigerate leftovers.

EASY LEMON PUDDING

Makes 6 to 8 servings

1 (14-ounce) can Eagle® Brand
    Sweetened Condensed Milk
    (NOT evaporated milk)
2½ cups cold water
2 (4-serving size) packages *instant*
    lemon flavor pudding mix

In large bowl, combine sweetened
condensed milk and water. Add
pudding mix; beat well. Chill. Serve in
individual dessert dishes or fill 12
medium-size cream puffs. Refrigerate
leftovers.

CRUNCHY LEMON SQUARES

Makes 9 servings

1 cup unsifted flour
1 cup quick-cooking oats
½ cup coarsely chopped pecans
½ cup firmly packed light brown
    sugar
½ cup flaked coconut
1 teaspoon baking powder
½ cup margarine or butter, melted
1 (14-ounce) can Eagle® Brand
    Sweetened Condensed Milk
    (NOT evaporated milk)
½ cup ReaLemon® Lemon Juice from
    Concentrate
1 tablespoon grated lemon rind

Preheat oven to 350° (325° for glass
dish). In medium bowl, combine flour,
oats, nuts, sugar, coconut, baking
powder and margarine; stir until
crumbly. Reserving half the crumb
mixture, press remainder evenly on
bottom of 9-inch square baking pan. In
medium bowl, combine sweetened
condensed milk, ReaLemon® brand and
rind; spread into prepared pan. Sprinkle
with reserved crumb mixture. Bake 25 to
30 minutes or until lightly browned.
Cool. Chill. Cut into squares. Garnish
as desired. Refrigerate leftovers.

BUTTERSCOTCH APPLE SQUARES

Makes 12 servings

¼ cup margarine or butter
1½ cups graham cracker crumbs
2 small all-purpose apples, pared and chopped (about 1¼ cups)
1 (6-ounce) package butterscotch-flavored chips
1 (14-ounce) can Eagle® Brand Sweetened Condensed Milk (NOT evaporated milk)
1 (3½-ounce) can flaked coconut (1⅓ cups)
1 cup chopped nuts

Preheat oven to 350° (325° for glass dish). In 13×9-inch baking pan, melt margarine in oven. Sprinkle crumbs evenly over margarine; top with apples. In heavy saucepan, over medium heat, melt chips with sweetened condensed milk. Pour butterscotch mixture evenly over apples. Top with coconut and nuts; press down firmly. Bake 25 to 30 minutes or until lightly browned. Cool. Cut into squares. Garnish as desired. Refrigerate leftovers.

MICROWAVE: In 12×17-inch baking dish, melt margarine on 100% power (high) 1 minute. Sprinkle crumbs evenly over margarine; top with apples. In 1-quart glass measure, melt chips with sweetened condensed milk on 70% power (medium-high) 2 to 3 minutes. Stir until smooth. Pour butterscotch mixture evenly over apples. Top with coconut and nuts. Press down firmly. Cook on 100% power (high) 8 to 9 minutes. Proceed as above.

FUDGY MILK CHOCOLATE FONDUE

Makes about 3 cups

1 (16-ounce) can chocolate-flavored
   syrup
1 (14-ounce) can Eagle® Brand
   Sweetened Condensed Milk
   (NOT evaporated milk)
   Dash salt
1½ teaspoons vanilla extract
   Dippers

In heavy saucepan, combine syrup, sweetened condensed milk and salt. Over medium heat, cook and stir 12 to 15 minutes or until slightly thickened. Remove from heat; stir in vanilla. Serve warm with Dippers. Refrigerate leftovers.

Dippers: Pound cake cubes, cherries with stems, orange sections, melon balls, pineapple chunks, strawberries, banana slices, apple wedges, grapes, dried apricots, peach chunks, plum slices, pear slices, angel food cake cubes, kiwifruit slices and marshmallows.

Tip: Can be served warm or cold over ice cream. Can be made several weeks ahead. Store tightly covered in refrigerator.

MICROWAVE: In 1-quart glass measure, combine syrup, sweetened condensed milk and salt. Cook on 100% power (high) 3½ to 4 minutes, stirring after 2 minutes. Stir in vanilla.

CREAMY APRICOT SNACK SPREAD

Makes about 3½ cups

1 (14-ounce) can Eagle® Brand Sweetened Condensed Milk (NOT evaporated milk)
2 cups finely chopped dried apricots or dates
¾ cup finely chopped nuts
1 teaspoon vanilla extract

In heavy saucepan, over medium heat, combine sweetened condensed milk and apricots; cook and stir until thickened, about 8 minutes. Remove from heat; stir in nuts and vanilla. Serve as a spread with plain or cheese crackers or cookies. Store covered at room temperature.

MICROWAVE: In 1-quart glass measure, combine sweetened condensed milk and apricots. Cook on 50% power (medium) 5 to 6 minutes, stirring after 3 minutes. Stir in nuts and vanilla. Proceed as above.

GOLDEN BREAD PUDDING

Makes 6 to 8 servings

4 cups soft white bread cubes (5 slices)
3 eggs
1 teaspoon ground cinnamon
3 cups warm water
1 (14-ounce) can Eagle® Brand Sweetened Condensed Milk (NOT evaporated milk)
2 tablespoons margarine or butter, melted
2 teaspoons vanilla extract
½ teaspoon salt

Preheat oven to 350°. Place bread cubes in buttered 9-inch square baking pan. In large bowl, beat eggs and cinnamon; stir in remaining ingredients. Pour evenly over bread, completely moistening bread. Bake 45 to 50 minutes or until knife inserted in center comes out clean. Cool. Serve warm or chilled. Refrigerate leftovers.

Tip: For a softer, more custard-like bread pudding, decrease bread cubes to 3 cups (4 slices bread).

Apple Bread Pudding: Arrange 2 cups pared, chopped all-purpose apples (3 medium) and ½ cup raisins, then bread in baking pan. Increase margarine to ¼ cup. Reduce water to 1¾ cups. Proceed as above.

Pineapple Bread Pudding: Add 1 (8- or 8¼-ounce) can crushed pineapple, undrained, to bread cubes. Reduce water to 2¾ cups. Proceed as above.

Blueberry 'n' Spice Bread Pudding: Add 2 cups fresh *or* thawed dry-pack frozen blueberries to bread cubes. Increase margarine to ¼ cup. Add ½ teaspoon ground cinnamon and ½ teaspoon ground nutmeg. Reduce water to 1½ cups. Proceed as above.

CHOCOLATE BANANA CREAM DESSERT

Makes 10 to 12 servings

1 (14-ounce) can Eagle® Brand
    Sweetened Condensed Milk
    (NOT evaporated milk)
2 (1-ounce) squares unsweetened
    chocolate, melted
1½ cups cold water
1 (4-serving size) package *instant*
    chocolate flavor pudding mix
1 teaspoon vanilla extract
2 cups (1 pint) Borden® Whipping
    Cream, whipped
¾ cup chopped pecans, toasted if
    desired
1 (9- or 10-ounce) prepared angel food
    cake, torn into small pieces
    (about 6 cups)
4 bananas, sliced

In large mixer bowl, beat sweetened
condensed milk and chocolate until
smooth. Add water, pudding mix and
vanilla; beat well. Chill 5 minutes. Fold
in whipped cream and ½ *cup* pecans.
Spoon 2 cups pudding mixture into 3- to
4-quart glass serving bowl *or* 13×9-inch
dish; top with half *each* cake, bananas
and remaining pudding mixture. Repeat
layering, ending with pudding mixture.
Garnish with remaining ¼ *cup* pecans.
Cover; chill. Refrigerate leftovers.

FRUITED AMBROSIA ▲

Makes 10 to 12 servings

1 (14-ounce) can Eagle® Brand
    Sweetened Condensed Milk
    (NOT evaporated milk)
1 (8-ounce) container Borden® Lite-
    line® Plain Yogurt
½ cup ReaLime® Lime Juice from
    Concentrate
2 (11-ounce) cans mandarin orange
    segments, drained
1 (20-ounce) can pineapple chunks,
    drained
1½ cups grape halves (about ½ pound)
1 (3½-ounce) can flaked coconut
    (1⅓ cups)
1 cup Campfire® Miniature
    Marshmallows
1 cup chopped pecans or walnuts
½ cup sliced maraschino cherries,
    well drained

In large bowl, combine sweetened
condensed milk, yogurt and ReaLime®
brand; mix well. Stir in remaining
ingredients. Chill 3 hours or longer to
blend flavors. Garnish as desired.
Refrigerate leftovers.

APPLE STREUSEL SQUARES

Makes 6 to 8 servings

5 medium all-purpose apples, pared, cored and sliced (about 5 cups)
1 (14-ounce) can Eagle® Brand Sweetened Condensed Milk (NOT evaporated milk)
1 teaspoon ground cinnamon
½ cup plus 2 tablespoons cold margarine or butter
1½ cups biscuit baking mix
½ cup firmly packed brown sugar
½ cup chopped nuts

Preheat oven to 325°. In medium bowl, combine apples, sweetened condensed milk and cinnamon. In large bowl, cut *½ cup* margarine into *1 cup* biscuit mix until crumbly. Stir in apple mixture. Pour into ungreased 9-inch square baking pan. In small bowl, combine remaining *½ cup* biscuit mix and sugar; cut in remaining *2 tablespoons* margarine until crumbly. Add nuts. Sprinkle evenly over apple mixture. Bake 1 hour or until golden brown. Serve warm with ice cream or whipped topping if desired.

MICROWAVE: In 2-quart round baking dish, prepare as above. Cook on 100% power (high) 14 to 15 minutes, rotating dish after 7 minutes. Let stand 5 minutes.

BAKED ALMOND PUDDING

Makes 8 to 10 servings

¼ cup firmly packed brown sugar
¾ cup slivered almonds, toasted
1 (14-ounce) can Eagle® Brand
    Sweetened Condensed Milk
    (NOT evaporated milk)
5 eggs
1 cup (½ pint) Borden® Whipping
    Cream
¼ cup water
½ teaspoon almond extract
    Additional toasted almonds,
    optional

Preheat oven to 325°. In 8-inch round layer cake pan, sprinkle sugar; set aside. In blender or food processor container, grind nuts; add sweetened condensed milk, eggs, ½ *cup* cream, water and extract. Blend thoroughly. Pour into prepared pan; set in larger pan. Fill larger pan with 1 inch hot water. Bake 40 to 45 minutes or until knife inserted near center comes out clean. Cool. Chill; invert onto serving plate. Beat remaining cream for garnish; top with additional almonds if desired. Refrigerate leftovers.

CARAMEL FLAN

Makes 10 to 12 servings

¾ cup sugar
4 eggs
1¾ cups water
1 (14-ounce) can Eagle® Brand
    Sweetened Condensed Milk
    (NOT evaporated milk)
½ teaspoon vanilla extract
⅛ teaspoon salt

Preheat oven to 350°. In heavy skillet, over medium heat, cook sugar, stirring constantly until melted and caramel-colored. Pour into ungreased 9-inch round or square baking pan, tilting to coat bottom completely. In medium bowl, beat eggs; stir in water, sweetened condensed milk, vanilla and salt. Pour over caramelized sugar; set pan in larger pan (a broiler pan). Fill larger pan with 1 inch hot water. Bake 55 to 60 minutes or until knife inserted near center comes out clean. Cool. Chill. Loosen side of flan with knife; invert onto serving plate with rim. Garnish as desired. Refrigerate leftovers.

FRUIT GLAZED BAKED CUSTARDS

Makes 6 servings

3 eggs
1 (14-ounce) can Eagle® Brand
    Sweetened Condensed Milk
    (NOT evaporated milk)
1 cup water
1 teaspoon vanilla extract
½ cup red currant jelly
2 tablespoons orange-flavored
    liqueur *or* orange juice
1 tablespoon cornstarch
    Few drops red food coloring,
    optional
    Fresh strawberries or other fruit

Preheat oven to 350°. In medium bowl, beat eggs; stir in sweetened condensed milk, water and vanilla. Pour equal portions of mixture into 6 lightly greased 6-ounce custard cups. Set cups in shallow pan; fill pan with 1 inch hot water. Bake 45 to 50 minutes or until knife inserted in center comes out clean. Cool. In small saucepan, combine jelly, liqueur and cornstarch. Cook and stir until jelly melts and mixture comes to a boil. Stir in food coloring if desired. Cool to room temperature. Invert custards onto serving plates. Top with sauce and strawberries. Refrigerate leftovers.

TOP TO BOTTOM: BAKED ALMOND PUDDING, CARAMEL FLAN, FRUIT GLAZED BAKED CUSTARDS

ORANGE NUT CREAM DESSERTS ▲

Makes 6 to 8 servings

1 (14-ounce) can Eagle® Brand
    Sweetened Condensed Milk
    (NOT evaporated milk)
1 (6-ounce) can frozen orange juice
    concentrate, thawed
1 (8-ounce) container Borden® Sour
    Cream
1 cup flaked coconut
½ cup chopped pecans
1 tablespoon grated orange rind
    Fresh orange sections

In medium bowl, combine sweetened condensed milk and juice concentrate. Stir in sour cream. In small bowl, combine coconut, nuts and rind. Layer filling, coconut mixture then orange sections in dessert dishes. Repeat, ending with coconut mixture and orange sections. Chill. Refrigerate leftovers.

LEMON CHIFFON LOAF

Makes 6 to 8 servings

24 ladyfinger halves
1 (14-ounce) can Eagle® Brand
    Sweetened Condensed Milk
    (NOT evaporated milk)
⅓ cup ReaLemon® Lemon Juice from
    Concentrate
    Yellow food coloring, optional
3 egg whites*
¼ teaspoon cream of tartar
1 cup (½ pint) Borden® Whipping
    Cream, stiffly whipped

Line bottom and sides of 9×5-inch loaf pan with aluminum foil, extending foil 1 inch beyond edge of pan. Line sides of pan with *18 ladyfinger halves*. In large bowl, combine sweetened condensed milk, ReaLemon® brand and food coloring if desired; mix well. In small mixer bowl, beat egg whites with cream of tartar until stiff but not dry; fold into sweetened condensed milk mixture. Fold in whipped cream. Pour into prepared pan. Cover filling with remaining *6 ladyfinger halves*. Cover. Chill 4 hours or until set. Invert onto serving plate; peel off foil. Garnish as desired. Refrigerate leftovers.

*Use only Grade A clean, uncracked eggs.

CREAMY BANANA PUDDING

Makes 8 to 10 servings

1 (14-ounce) can Eagle® Brand
  Sweetened Condensed Milk
  (NOT evaporated milk)
1½ cups cold water
1 (4-serving size) package *instant*
  vanilla flavor pudding mix
2 cups (1 pint) Borden® Whipping
  Cream, whipped
36 vanilla wafers
3 medium bananas, sliced and
  dipped in ReaLemon® Lemon
  Juice from Concentrate

In large bowl, combine sweetened condensed milk and water. Add pudding mix; beat well. Chill 5 minutes. Fold in whipped cream. Spoon *1 cup* pudding mixture into 2½-quart glass serving bowl. Top with one-third *each* of the wafers, bananas and pudding. Repeat layering twice, ending with pudding. Chill. Garnish as desired. Refrigerate leftovers.

Tip: Mixture can be layered in individual serving dishes.

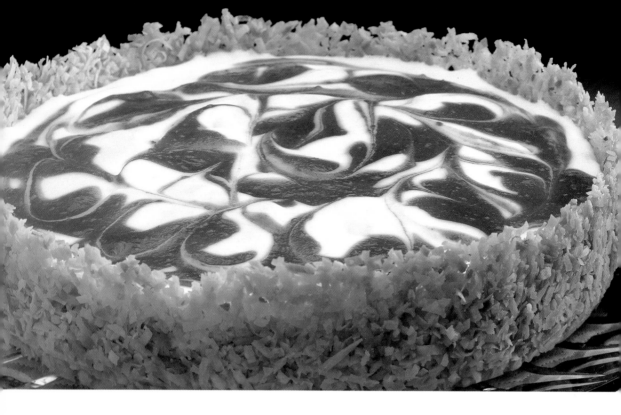

RASPBERRY SWIRL DESSERT

Makes 10 to 12 servings

1 (7-ounce) package flaked coconut, toasted (2⅔ cups)

⅓ cup margarine or butter, melted

1 (10-ounce) package frozen red raspberries in syrup, thawed

1 tablespoon cornstarch

1 envelope unflavored gelatine

¼ cup water

1 (14-ounce) can Eagle® Brand Sweetened Condensed Milk (NOT evaporated milk)

1 (8-ounce) container Borden® Sour Cream

3 tablespoons orange-flavored liqueur

1 cup (½ pint) Borden® Whipping Cream, stiffly whipped

Combine coconut and margarine; press firmly on bottom and up side of 8- or 9-inch springform pan. Chill. In blender container, puree raspberries. In small saucepan, combine pureed raspberries and cornstarch; cook and stir until mixture thickens. Cool to room temperature. Meanwhile, in small saucepan, sprinkle gelatine over water; let stand 1 minute. Over low heat, stir until gelatine dissolves. In large bowl, combine sweetened condensed milk, sour cream, liqueur and gelatine; mix well. Fold in whipped cream. Chill 10 minutes or until mixture mounds slightly. Spread half the gelatine mixture into prepared pan; top with half the raspberry mixture in small amounts. Repeat layering. With metal spatula, swirl raspberry mixture through cream mixture. Chill 6 hours or until set. Garnish as desired. Refrigerate leftovers.

Raspberry Swirl Charlotte: Omit coconut and margarine. Line bottom and side of springform pan with 28 ladyfinger halves. Proceed as above.

CHOCOLATE CINNAMON BREAD PUDDING

Makes 6 to 8 servings

4 cups soft white bread cubes (5 slices)
½ cup chopped nuts
3 eggs
¼ cup unsweetened cocoa
2 teaspoons vanilla extract
1 teaspoon ground cinnamon
½ teaspoon salt
1 (14-ounce) can Eagle® Brand Sweetened Condensed Milk (NOT evaporated milk)
2¾ cups water
2 tablespoons margarine or butter, melted
Cinnamon Cream Sauce

Preheat oven to 350°. Place bread cubes and nuts in buttered 9-inch square baking pan. In large bowl, beat eggs, cocoa, vanilla, cinnamon and salt. Add sweetened condensed milk; mix well. Stir in water and margarine. Pour evenly over bread mixture, completely moistening bread. Bake 40 to 45 minutes or until knife inserted in center comes out clean. Cool slightly. Serve warm with Cinnamon Cream Sauce. Refrigerate leftovers.

Cinnamon Cream Sauce: In medium saucepan, combine 1 cup (½ pint) Borden® Whipping Cream, ⅔ cup firmly packed brown sugar, 1 teaspoon vanilla and ½ teaspoon ground cinnamon. Bring to a boil; reduce heat and boil rapidly 6 to 8 minutes or until thickened, stirring occasionally. Cool slightly. Serve warm. (Makes about 1 cup)

CREAMY PECAN RUM SAUCE

Makes about 1½ cups

¼ cup margarine or butter
1 (14-ounce) can Eagle® Brand Sweetened Condensed Milk (NOT evaporated milk)
½ teaspoon rum flavoring
Dash salt
¼ cup chopped pecans

In small saucepan, over medium heat, melt margarine; add remaining ingredients. Cook and stir until slightly thickened, 10 to 12 minutes. Cool 10 minutes (*sauce thickens as it cools*). Serve warm over baked apples, fruit or ice cream. Refrigerate leftovers.

To Reheat: In small heavy saucepan, combine desired amount of sauce with small amount of water. Over low heat, stir constantly until heated through.

MICROWAVE: In 1-quart glass measure, melt margarine on 100% power (high) 1 minute. Stir in remaining ingredients. Cook on 70% power (medium-high) 3 to 3½ minutes. Proceed as above.

CREAMY PECAN RUM SAUCE

FLOATING ISLAND LIME DESSERTS

Makes 4 servings

Floating Islands
1 (14-ounce) can Eagle® Brand Sweetened Condensed Milk (NOT evaporated milk)
2 egg yolks*
½ cup ReaLime® Lime Juice from Concentrate
2 to 3 drops green food coloring, optional
2 tablespoons flaked coconut, toasted

Prepare Floating Islands. Meanwhile, in medium bowl, beat sweetened condensed milk and egg yolks; stir in ReaLime® brand and food coloring if desired. Spoon into four 6-ounce dessert dishes. Top each with a Floating Island. Chill 2 hours or until set. Garnish with coconut. Refrigerate leftovers.

FLOATING ISLAND LIME DESSERT

Floating Islands: In small mixer bowl, beat 2 egg whites* until soft peaks form. Gradually beat in 2 tablespoons sugar, beating until stiff but not dry. Drop one-fourth of mixture onto simmering water in large skillet; repeat to make 4 islands. Simmer uncovered 5 minutes or until meringues are set. Remove with slotted spoon; drain on paper towels.

*Use only Grade A clean, uncracked eggs.

FRENCH APPLE BREAD PUDDING

Makes 6 to 8 servings

3 eggs
1 (14-ounce) can Eagle® Brand Sweetened Condensed Milk (NOT evaporated milk)
3 medium all-purpose apples, pared, cored and finely chopped (about 2 cups)
1¾ cups hot water
¼ cup margarine or butter, melted
1 teaspoon ground cinnamon
1 teaspoon vanilla extract
4 cups French bread cubes (about 6 ounces)
½ cup raisins, optional
Whipped cream

Preheat oven to 350°. In large bowl, beat eggs; add sweetened condensed milk, apples, water, margarine, cinnamon and vanilla. Stir in bread and raisins, completely moistening bread. Turn into buttered 9-inch square baking pan. Bake 1 hour or until knife inserted near center comes out clean. Cool. Serve warm with whipped cream. Garnish as desired. Refrigerate leftovers.

SPICY CARAMEL SAUCE

Makes about 1¼ cups

**1 (14-ounce) can Eagle® Brand
Sweetened Condensed Milk
(NOT evaporated milk)**
2 to 4 teaspoons water
½ teaspoon ground cinnamon
¼ teaspoon almond extract

Caramelize sweetened condensed milk.
Add remaining ingredients; mix well.
Serve warm over ice cream, cake, baked
apples or apple dumplings. Refrigerate
leftovers.

TO CARAMELIZE EAGLE® BRAND SWEETENED CONDENSED MILK

Oven Method: Preheat oven to 425°.
Pour sweetened condensed milk into
8- or 9-inch pie plate. Cover with
aluminum foil; place in shallow pan. Fill
pan with hot water. Bake 1 to 1½ hours
or until thick and light caramel-colored.

Microwave Method: Pour sweetened
condensed milk into 2-quart glass
measure. Cook on 50% power (medium)
4 minutes, stirring briskly every 2
minutes until smooth. Cook on 30%
power (medium-low) 12 to 18 minutes
or until thick and light caramel-colored,
stirring briskly every 2 minutes until
smooth.

**CAUTION: NEVER HEAT
UNOPENED CAN.**

BERRY BANANA TRIFLE

Makes 8 to 10 servings

1 (10-ounce) package frozen red
    raspberries in syrup, thawed and
    drained, reserving ⅔ cup syrup
¼ cup red currant or strawberry jelly
1 tablespoon cornstarch
1 (14-ounce) can Eagle® Brand
    Sweetened Condensed Milk
    (NOT evaporated milk)
1½ cups cold water
1 (4-serving size) package *instant*
    vanilla flavor pudding mix
2 cups (1 pint) Borden® Whipping
    Cream, whipped
1 (3-ounce) package ladyfingers,
    split, *or* 1 (10¾-ounce) loaf pound
    cake, cut into 12 slices then each
    slice cut in half vertically
3 medium bananas, sliced and
    dipped in ReaLemon® Lemon
    Juice from Concentrate
1 cup coarsely chopped walnuts,
    toasted

In small saucepan, combine ⅔ *cup* reserved raspberry syrup, jelly and cornstarch. Cook and stir until thickened and clear. Stir in raspberries. Cool. In large bowl, combine sweetened condensed milk and water. Add pudding mix; beat well. Chill 5 minutes. Fold in whipped cream. Spoon half the pudding mixture into 2½- to 3-quart glass serving bowl. Line side of bowl with ladyfingers; arrange remaining ladyfingers on top of pudding. Top with half *each* of the bananas, raspberry sauce and walnuts. Repeat with remaining ingredients. Garnish as desired. Refrigerate leftovers.

BERRIES 'N' BITS PUDDING

Makes 8 to 10 servings

1 (14-ounce) can Eagle® Brand
    Sweetened Condensed Milk
    (NOT evaporated milk)
1½ cups cold water
  1 (4-serving size) package *instant*
    vanilla flavor pudding mix
  2 cups (1 pint) Borden® Whipping
    Cream, whipped
 36 vanilla wafers
  1 quart fresh strawberries, hulled
    and sliced
 ¾ cup mini chocolate chips
    Additional mini chocolate chips,
    vanilla wafers and strawberries,
    optional

In large bowl, combine sweetened
condensed milk and water. Add
pudding mix; beat well. Chill 5 minutes.
Fold in whipped cream. Spoon *2 cups*
pudding into 3-quart glass serving bowl;
top with half each of the vanilla wafers,
strawberries, mini chocolate chips and
remaining pudding. Repeat layering.
Garnish with additional mini chocolate
chips, vanilla wafers and strawberries if
desired. Chill. Refrigerate leftovers.

QUICK 'N' CREAMY PUDDING

Makes 8 to 10 servings

1 (14-ounce) can Eagle® Brand
    Sweetened Condensed Milk
    (NOT evaporated milk)
2½ cups cold water
  2 (4-serving size) packages *instant*
    pudding mix, any flavor
  1 cup (½ pint) Borden® Whipping
    Cream, whipped, *or* 1 (4-ounce)
    container frozen non-dairy
    whipped topping, thawed

In large bowl, combine sweetened
condensed milk and water. Add
pudding mix; beat well. Fold in
whipped cream. Spoon into individual
serving dishes. Chill. Refrigerate
leftovers.

PUMPKIN RUM CUSTARDS

Makes 8 to 10 servings

1 cup sugar
4 eggs
1 (14-ounce) can Eagle® Brand
  Sweetened Condensed Milk
  (NOT evaporated milk)
1½ cups water
1 (16-ounce) can pumpkin (2 cups)
⅓ cup light rum
½ teaspoon ground nutmeg
½ teaspoon salt
⅛ to ¼ teaspoon ground ginger

Preheat oven to 350°. In heavy skillet, over medium heat, cook sugar, stirring constantly until melted and caramel-colored. Using eight to ten 6-ounce custard cups, pour about 1 tablespoon caramelized sugar on bottom of each. In large mixer bowl, beat eggs; add remaining ingredients. Pour equal portions into prepared cups. Set cups in shallow pan; fill pan with 1 inch hot water. Bake 50 to 60 minutes or until knife inserted in center comes out clean. Cool. Chill. Invert custards onto serving plates. Garnish as desired. Refrigerate leftovers.

SOUTHERN YAM DESSERT SQUARES

Makes 8 to 10 servings

2 cups quick-cooking oats
1½ cups unsifted flour
½ teaspoon baking soda
½ teaspoon salt
1 cup margarine or butter, softened
1 cup firmly packed light brown
  sugar
1 teaspoon vanilla extract
½ cup chopped nuts
1 pound yams or sweet potatoes,
  cooked, peeled and mashed
  (about 2 cups)
1 (14-ounce) can Eagle® Brand
  Sweetened Condensed Milk
  (NOT evaporated milk)
2 eggs, beaten
1½ teaspoons ground allspice or
  pumpkin pie spice
1 teaspoon grated orange rind

Preheat oven to 350°. Combine oats, flour, baking soda and salt; set aside. In large mixer bowl, beat margarine, sugar and vanilla until fluffy. Add dry ingredients; mix until crumbly. Reserving 1 cup crumb mixture, press remainder firmly on bottom of 13×9-inch baking dish. Bake 10 minutes. Meanwhile, stir nuts into reserved crumb mixture. In large mixer bowl, beat remaining ingredients until well blended. Pour over prepared crust. Top with reserved crumb mixture. Bake 25 to 30 minutes or until golden brown. Cool. Serve warm or chilled. Garnish as desired. Refrigerate leftovers.

Tip: 1 (16- or 17-ounce) can sweet potatoes, drained and mashed, or 1 (16-ounce) can pumpkin can be substituted for yams.

STRAWBERRY CHIFFON SQUARES

Makes 10 to 12 servings

1½ cups vanilla wafer crumbs (about 45 wafers)
⅓ cup margarine or butter, melted
1 (4-serving size) package strawberry flavor gelatin
¾ cup boiling water
1 (14-ounce) can Eagle® Brand Sweetened Condensed Milk (NOT evaporated milk)
1 (10-ounce) package frozen sliced strawberries in syrup, thawed
4 cups Campfire® Miniature Marshmallows
1 cup (½ pint) Borden® Whipping Cream, whipped

Combine crumbs and margarine; press firmly on bottom of 9-inch square *or* 12×7-inch baking dish. In large bowl, dissolve gelatin in water; stir in sweetened condensed milk and strawberries. Fold in marshmallows and whipped cream. Pour into prepared dish. Chill 2 hours or until set. Garnish as desired. Refrigerate leftovers.

LIME CHIFFON SQUARES

Makes 10 to 12 servings

1 cup graham cracker crumbs
¼ cup margarine or butter, melted
1 (4-serving size) package lime flavor gelatin
1 cup boiling water
1 (14-ounce) can Eagle® Brand Sweetened Condensed Milk (NOT evaporated milk)
1 (8- or 8¼-ounce) can crushed pineapple, undrained
2 tablespoons ReaLime® Lime Juice from Concentrate
4 cups Campfire® Miniature Marshmallows
1 cup (½ pint) Borden® Whipping Cream, whipped

Combine crumbs and margarine; press firmly on bottom of 9-inch square *or* 12×7-inch baking dish. In large bowl, dissolve gelatin in water; stir in sweetened condensed milk, pineapple and ReaLime® brand. Fold in marshmallows and whipped cream. Pour into prepared dish. Chill 2 hours or until set. Garnish as desired. Refrigerate leftovers.

LIME CHIFFON SQUARE

BUTTERSCOTCH APPLE DIP

Makes about 1¾ cups

1 (6-ounce) package butterscotch-flavored chips
1 (14-ounce) can Eagle® Brand Sweetened Condensed Milk (NOT evaporated milk)
¼ teaspoon salt
2 teaspoons white vinegar
¼ to ½ teaspoon ground cinnamon Apple wedges

In heavy saucepan, over low heat, melt chips with sweetened condensed milk and salt. Remove from heat; stir in vinegar and cinnamon. Serve warm with apples. Refrigerate leftovers.

Tip: Can be served warm as an ice cream topping.

MICROWAVE: In 1-quart glass measure, combine sweetened condensed milk, chips and salt. Cook on 100% power (high) 3 to 3½ minutes, stirring after 2 minutes. Stir in vinegar and cinnamon.

CREAMY LEMON FRUIT SAUCE

Makes about 3 cups

1 (14-ounce) can Eagle® Brand Sweetened Condensed Milk (NOT evaporated milk)
1 (6-ounce) can frozen lemonade concentrate, thawed
2 tablespoons kirsch or other cherry-flavored liqueur
1 (4-ounce) container frozen non-dairy whipped topping, thawed
1 teaspoon grated lemon rind, optional
Assorted fresh fruit (apples, bananas, strawberries, grapes, pineapple, etc.)

In medium bowl, combine all ingredients except whipped topping and fruit; fold in whipped topping. Serve with fruit. Refrigerate leftovers.

BUTTERSCOTCH APPLE DIP

CREAMY RICE PUDDING

Makes 4 to 6 servings

2½ cups water
½ cup uncooked long grain rice
1 cinnamon stick *or* ¼ teaspoon
    ground cinnamon
2 (½-inch) pieces lemon rind
    Dash salt
1 (14-ounce) can Eagle® Brand
    Sweetened Condensed Milk
    (NOT evaporated milk)
    Additional ground cinnamon

In medium saucepan, combine water, rice, cinnamon, lemon rind and salt; let stand 30 minutes. Bring to a boil, stirring occasionally. Add sweetened condensed milk; mix well. Return to a boil; stir. Reduce heat to medium. Cook uncovered, stirring frequently, until liquid is absorbed to top of rice, about 15 minutes. Cool (pudding thickens as it cools). Remove cinnamon stick and lemon rind. Sprinkle with additional cinnamon. Serve warm or chilled. Refrigerate leftovers.

STRAWBERRIES ROMANOFF

Makes 10 to 12 servings

1 (14-ounce) can Eagle® Brand
    Sweetened Condensed Milk
    (NOT evaporated milk)
1 cup water
3 to 4 tablespoons orange-flavored
    liqueur *or* kirsch
1 (4-serving size) package *instant*
    vanilla flavor pudding mix
2 cups (1 pint) Borden® Whipping
    Cream, *stiffly whipped*
1 quart fresh strawberries, hulled
    and sliced

In large bowl, combine sweetened condensed milk, water and liqueur. Add pudding mix; beat well. Chill 15 minutes. Fold in whipped cream. Cover and chill. Just before serving, reserve *1 cup* strawberries; fold in remaining strawberries. Garnish with reserved strawberries. Refrigerate leftovers.

CHERRY ALMOND CREAM DESSERT

Makes 10 to 12 servings

1 (14-ounce) can Eagle® Brand
    Sweetened Condensed Milk
    (NOT evaporated milk)
1½ cups cold water
1 (4-serving size) *instant* vanilla
    flavor pudding mix
1 teaspoon almond extract
2 cups (1 pint) Borden® Whipping
    Cream, whipped
1 (10¾ *or* 12-ounce) prepared loaf
    pound cake, cut into 10 slices
1 (21-ounce) can cherry pie filling,
    chilled
    Toasted almonds

In large bowl, combine sweetened condensed milk and water. Add pudding mix and extract; beat well. Chill 5 minutes. Fold in whipped cream. Spoon half the cream mixture into 13×9-inch baking dish; top with cake slices, pie filling, remaining cream mixture then almonds. Chill. Refrigerate leftovers.

PEACH MELBA TRIFLE

Makes 10 to 12 servings

1 (14-ounce) can Eagle® Brand Sweetened Condensed Milk (NOT evaporated milk)
1½ cups cold water
1 (4-serving size) package *instant* vanilla flavor pudding mix
2 cups (1 pint) Borden® Whipping Cream, whipped
¼ cup plus 1 tablespoon dry sherry *or* orange juice
1 (9- or 10-ounce) prepared angel food cake, torn into small pieces (about 6 cups)
1½ pounds fresh peaches, pared and sliced, *or* 1 (29-ounce) can sliced peaches, drained
½ cup red raspberry preserves
Toasted almonds and additional preserves, optional

In large bowl, combine sweetened condensed milk and water. Add pudding mix; beat well. Chill 5 minutes. Fold in whipped cream and *1 tablespoon* sherry. Place about *4 cups* cake pieces in 3- to 4-quart glass serving bowl. Sprinkle with *2 tablespoons* sherry. Top with half the peach slices, *½ cup* preserves and half the pudding mixture. Repeat layering with remaining cake, sherry, peach slices and pudding mixture. Garnish with almonds and preserves if desired. Chill. Refrigerate leftovers.

FRESH STRAWBERRY TRIFLE

Makes 10 to 12 servings

24 ladyfinger halves
1 quart fresh strawberries, hulled and sliced
¼ cup dry sherry
1 (14-ounce) can Eagle® Brand Sweetened Condensed Milk (NOT evaporated milk)
⅓ cup ReaLemon® Lemon Juice from Concentrate
2 cups (1 pint) Borden® Whipping Cream, whipped

Line bottom and side of 2-quart glass serving bowl with ladyfinger halves. Spoon *1½ cups* sliced strawberries over bottom; sprinkle with *2 tablespoons* sherry. In large bowl, combine sweetened condensed milk, ReaLemon® brand and *1½ cups* sliced strawberries; mix well. Reserving about *1 cup* whipped cream, fold remaining whipped cream and remaining *2 tablespoons* sherry into strawberry mixture. Spoon into prepared bowl. Chill. Top with remaining strawberries and reserved whipped cream. Refrigerate leftovers.

PEACH MELBA TRIFLE (TOP), FRESH STRAWBERRY TRIFLE (BOTTOM)

LEMON CRUNCH PARFAITS

Makes 4 to 6 servings

½ cup unsifted flour
¼ cup chopped nuts
2 tablespoons light brown sugar
¼ cup margarine or butter, melted
1 (14-ounce) can Eagle® Brand Sweetened Condensed Milk (NOT evaporated milk)
¼ cup ReaLemon® Lemon Juice from Concentrate
1 (8-ounce) container Borden® Lite-line® Lemon Yogurt
Few drops yellow food coloring, optional

Preheat oven to 350°. Combine flour, nuts, sugar and margarine. Spread in 8-inch square baking pan. Bake 10 minutes, stirring after 5 minutes. Cool. In medium bowl, combine sweetened condensed milk, ReaLemon® brand, yogurt and food coloring if desired. In parfait or dessert glasses, layer crumbs and yogurt mixture. Chill. Refrigerate leftovers.

FLUFFY YOGURT FRUIT DESSERTS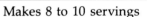

Makes 8 to 10 servings

1 (14-ounce) can Eagle® Brand Sweetened Condensed Milk (NOT evaporated milk)
1 (8-ounce) container Borden® Lite-line® Fruit Yogurt, any flavor
2 tablespoons ReaLemon® Lemon Juice from Concentrate
Food coloring, optional
2 cups fresh fruit
1 (8-ounce) container frozen non-dairy whipped topping, thawed

In large bowl, combine all ingredients except whipped topping; mix well. Fold in whipped topping. Spoon into individual serving dishes. Chill. Just before serving, garnish with additional fruit. Refrigerate leftovers.

POLYNESIAN CHOCOLATE CREPES

Makes 16 to 18 servings

Pineapple Cream Filling
3 eggs
¾ cup water
½ cup Borden® Coffee Cream *or* Half-and-Half
¾ cup plus 2 tablespoons unsifted flour
3 tablespoons unsweetened cocoa
2 tablespoons sugar
⅛ teaspoon salt
3 tablespoons margarine or butter, melted and cooled
Orange Fudge Topping

Prepare Pineapple Cream Filling; chill. In blender or food processor container, combine eggs, water and cream; blend 10 seconds. Add flour, cocoa, sugar, salt and margarine; blend until smooth. Let stand at room temperature 10 minutes. Lightly oil 6-inch crepe pan. Over medium heat, pour 2 to 3 tablespoons batter into pan. Lift and tilt pan to spread batter. Return to heat; cook until surface begins to dry. Loosen crepe around edges; turn and lightly cook other side. Invert pan over waxed paper; remove crepe. Repeat with remaining batter. Spoon about ¼ cup filling onto each crepe; roll up. Place seam-side down on serving plate. Serve with Orange Fudge Topping. Refrigerate leftovers.

Pineapple Cream Filling
1 (14-ounce) can Eagle® Brand Sweetened Condensed Milk (NOT evaporated milk)
1 (15¼-ounce) can crushed juice-pack pineapple, well drained
1 teaspoon grated orange rind
¼ cup orange juice
3 tablespoons ReaLemon® Lemon Juice from Concentrate
1 cup (½ pint) Borden® Whipping Cream, whipped

In medium bowl, combine all ingredients except whipped cream; mix well. Cover; chill at least 2 hours. Just before serving, fold in whipped cream. (Makes about 4 cups)

Orange Fudge Topping: In heavy saucepan, over low heat, melt 2 tablespoons margarine or butter; stir in ⅓ cup unsweetened cocoa. Add ¼ cup orange juice and 3 tablespoons water; mix well. Stir in 1 (14-ounce) can Eagle® Brand Sweetened Condensed Milk (NOT evaporated milk). Over medium heat, cook and stir until thickened and bubbly, about 5 minutes. Remove from heat; stir in 1 teaspoon vanilla extract. Serve warm. (Makes about 1½ cups)

HOT FUDGE SAUCE

Makes about 2 cups

1 (6-ounce) package semi-sweet chocolate chips *or* 4 (1-ounce) squares semi-sweet chocolate
2 tablespoons margarine or butter
1 (14-ounce) can Eagle® Brand Sweetened Condensed Milk (NOT evaporated milk)
2 tablespoons water
1 teaspoon vanilla extract

In heavy saucepan, over medium heat, melt chips and margarine with sweetened condensed milk, water and vanilla. Cook and stir constantly until thickened, about 5 minutes. Serve warm over ice cream. Refrigerate leftovers.

To Reheat: In small heavy saucepan, combine desired amount of sauce with small amount of water. Over low heat, stir constantly until heated through.

MICROWAVE: In 1-quart glass measure, combine ingredients. Cook on 100% power (high) 3 to 3½ minutes, stirring after each minute.

Variations:

Mocha: Add 1 teaspoon instant coffee. Proceed as above.

Toasted Almond: Omit vanilla extract. Add ½ teaspoon almond extract. When sauce is thickened, stir in ½ cup chopped toasted almonds.

Choco-Mint: Omit vanilla extract. Add ½ to 1 teaspoon peppermint extract. Proceed as above.

Spirited: Add ⅓ cup almond, coffee, mint *or* orange-flavored liqueur after mixture has thickened.

Mexican: Omit water. Add 2 tablespoons coffee-flavored liqueur *or* 1 teaspoon instant coffee dissolved in 2 tablespoons water, and 1 teaspoon ground cinnamon after mixture has thickened.

TOP TO BOTTOM: PEANUT BUTTER SAUCE, HOT FUDGE SAUCE, COCONUT PECAN SAUCE

PEANUT BUTTER SAUCE

Makes about 2 cups

**1 (14-ounce) can Eagle® Brand
Sweetened Condensed Milk
(NOT evaporated milk)**
⅓ cup peanut butter
⅓ cup chopped peanuts
1 teaspoon vanilla extract
½ teaspoon ground cinnamon

In heavy saucepan, over low heat, combine sweetened condensed milk and peanut butter; cook and stir until thickened. Remove from heat; stir in peanuts, vanilla and cinnamon. Serve warm over ice cream or with apples. Refrigerate leftovers.

To Reheat: In small heavy saucepan, combine desired amount of sauce with small amount of water. Over low heat, stir constantly until heated through.

MICROWAVE: In 1-quart glass measure, combine sweetened condensed milk and peanut butter. Cook on 100% power (high) 2½ to 3½ minutes, stirring after each minute. Proceed as above.

COCONUT PECAN SAUCE

Makes about 2 cups

**1 (14-ounce) can Eagle® Brand
Sweetened Condensed Milk
(NOT evaporated milk)**
2 egg yolks, beaten
¼ cup margarine or butter
½ cup flaked coconut
½ cup chopped pecans
1 teaspoon vanilla extract

In heavy saucepan, combine sweetened condensed milk, egg yolks and margarine. Over medium heat, cook and stir until thickened and bubbly, about 8 minutes. Stir in remaining ingredients. Serve warm over ice cream or cake. Refrigerate leftovers.

To Reheat: In small heavy saucepan, combine desired amount of sauce with small amount of water. Over low heat, stir constantly until heated through.

MICROWAVE: In 1-quart glass measure, combine sweetened condensed milk, egg yolks and margarine. Cook on 70% power (medium-high) 4 to 5 minutes, stirring after 3 minutes. Proceed as above.

CREAMY DUTCH APPLE DESSERT

Makes 10 to 12 servings

¼ cup margarine or butter
1½ cups graham cracker crumbs
**1 (14-ounce) can Eagle® Brand
Sweetened Condensed Milk
(NOT evaporated milk)**
**1 (8-ounce) container Borden® Sour
Cream**
**¼ cup ReaLemon® Lemon Juice from
Concentrate**
1 (21-ounce) can apple pie filling
¼ cup chopped walnuts
¼ teaspoon ground cinnamon

Preheat oven to 350°. In 10×6-inch baking dish, melt margarine in oven. Sprinkle crumbs over margarine; mix well and press firmly on bottom of dish. In medium bowl, combine sweetened condensed milk, sour cream and ReaLemon® brand; spread evenly over crumbs. Spoon pie filling evenly over creamy layer. Bake 25 to 30 minutes or until set. Cool slightly. Before serving, combine nuts and cinnamon; sprinkle over apple layer. Serve warm or chilled. Refrigerate leftovers.

APRICOT AMBROSIA DESSERT

Makes 8 to 10 servings

1 (30-ounce) can apricot halves, drained
1 (14-ounce) can Eagle® Brand Sweetened Condensed Milk (NOT evaporated milk)
⅓ cup ReaLemon® Lemon Juice from Concentrate
1 (8¼-ounce) can crushed pineapple, drained
½ cup slivered almonds, toasted and chopped
1 cup (½ pint) Borden® Whipping Cream, whipped
1 (3½-ounce) can flaked coconut, toasted (1⅓ cups)

Chop 6 apricot halves for garnish; set aside. In blender container, puree remaining apricots. In large bowl, combine sweetened condensed milk, ReaLemon® brand, pineapple and pureed apricots. Fold in almonds and whipped cream. In each individual serving dish, place 2 teaspoons coconut, then about ½ cup apricot mixture; top with reserved apricots and 2 teaspoons toasted coconut. Chill. Refrigerate leftovers.

APRICOT AMBROSIA DESSERT

Tip: Mixture can be prepared in a 1½-quart glass serving bowl. Layer one-half coconut mixture on bottom, apricot mixture, chopped apricots and remaining coconut.

OLD-FASHIONED BANANA PUDDING

Makes 6 to 8 servings

1 (14-ounce) can Eagle® Brand Sweetened Condensed Milk (NOT evaporated milk)
2 cups water
1 (4-serving size) package vanilla flavor pudding mix
2 eggs,* separated
36 vanilla wafers
3 bananas, sliced
¼ teaspoon cream of tartar
¼ cup sugar

Preheat oven to 400°. In medium saucepan, combine sweetened condensed milk and water; mix well. Stir in pudding mix and egg yolks. Over medium heat, cook and stir until thickened; remove from heat. Arrange layer of vanilla wafers on bottom and side of 1½-quart baking dish; top with half the bananas and half the pudding mixture. Repeat layering. In small mixer bowl, beat egg whites with cream of tartar until soft peaks form; gradually add sugar, beating until stiff but not dry. Spread on top of pudding, sealing to edge of dish. Bake 5 minutes or until lightly browned. Cool. Chill. Refrigerate leftovers.

*Use only Grade A clean, uncracked eggs.

QUICK CHOCOLATE MOUSSE ▲

Makes 8 to 10 servings

1 (14-ounce) can Eagle® Brand
  Sweetened Condensed Milk
  (NOT evaporated milk)
1 cup cold water
1 (4-serving size) package *instant*
  chocolate flavor pudding mix
1 cup (½ pint) Borden® Whipping
  Cream, whipped

In large bowl, combine sweetened
condensed milk and water. Add
pudding mix; beat well. Chill 5 minutes.
Fold in whipped cream. Spoon into
serving dishes; chill. Garnish as
desired. Refrigerate leftovers.

CHERRIES 'N' CREAM PARFAITS

Makes 6 to 8 servings

1 (14-ounce) can Eagle® Brand
  Sweetened Condensed Milk
  (NOT evaporated milk)
⅓ cup ReaLemon® Lemon Juice from
  Concentrate
1 (8-ounce) container Borden® Sour
  Cream
1 teaspoon almond extract
1 (21-ounce) can cherry pie filling,
  chilled

In medium bowl, combine sweetened
condensed milk and ReaLemon® brand.
Stir in sour cream and extract. Layer
cream mixture and pie filling in parfait
or dessert glasses, ending with pie
filling. Chill. Refrigerate leftovers.

ICE CREAM &
FROZEN DESSERTS

Top left: Easy Homemade
Vanilla Ice Cream
(recipe, page 155).
Top right: Easy Homemade
Chocolate Ice Cream.
Bottom left: Peppermint Ice
Cream Loaf (recipes, page 154)

BLACKBERRY-LEMON ICE CREAM

Makes about 2 quarts

- 3 cups (1½ pints) Borden® Half-and-Half
- 2 cups frozen unsweetened blackberries, mashed
- 1 (14-ounce) can Eagle® Brand Sweetened Condensed Milk (NOT evaporated milk)
- ¼ cup plus 2 tablespoons ReaLemon® Lemon Juice from Concentrate
- 1 teaspoon grated lemon rind, optional

In ice cream freezer container, combine ingredients; mix well. Freeze according to manufacturer's instructions. Return leftovers to freezer.

EASY HOMEMADE CHOCOLATE ICE CREAM

Makes about 1½ quarts

- 1 (14-ounce) can Eagle® Brand Sweetened Condensed Milk (NOT evaporated milk)
- ⅔ cup chocolate-flavored syrup
- 2 cups (1 pint) Borden® Whipping Cream, whipped (*do not use non-dairy whipped topping*)

In large bowl, combine sweetened condensed milk and syrup. Fold in whipped cream. Pour into 9 × 5-inch loaf pan or other 2-quart container; cover. Freeze 6 hours or until firm. Return leftovers to freezer.

Chocolate Mocha: Add 1 tablespoon instant coffee to sweetened condensed milk and syrup. Let stand 10 minutes. Proceed as above.

Chocolate Peanut Butter: Add ½ cup peanut butter. Proceed as above.

Chocolate Nut: Add ¾ cup chopped nuts. Proceed as above.

Chocolate Rocky Road: Add ½ cup chopped peanuts and 1 cup Campfire® Miniature Marshmallows. Proceed as above.

Chocolate Mint: Add 1 teaspoon peppermint extract. Proceed as above.

Chocolate Chocolate Chip: Add ¾ cup mini chocolate chips. Proceed as above.

PEPPERMINT ICE CREAM LOAF

Makes 8 to 10 servings

- 2 cups finely crushed creme-filled chocolate sandwich cookies (about 20 cookies)
- 3 tablespoons margarine or butter, melted
- 1 cup crushed hard peppermint candy
- ¼ cup water
- 1 (14-ounce) can Eagle® Brand Sweetened Condensed Milk (NOT evaporated milk)
- 1 to 2 drops red food coloring, optional
- 2 cups (1 pint) Borden® Whipping Cream, whipped (*do not use non-dairy whipped topping*)

Line 9×5-inch loaf pan with aluminum foil, extending foil above sides of pan. Combine crumbs and margarine; press firmly on bottom and halfway up sides of prepared pan. In blender container, blend ¼ *cup* peppermint candy and water until candy dissolves. In large mixer bowl, beat sweetened condensed milk, food coloring if desired, ½ *cup* crushed candy and peppermint liquid until well blended. Fold in whipped cream and remaining ¼ *cup* crushed candy. Pour into prepared pan. Cover; freeze 6 hours or overnight. To serve, remove from pan; peel off foil and slice. Garnish as desired. Return leftovers to freezer.

EASY HOMEMADE VANILLA ICE CREAM

Makes about 1½ quarts

1 (14-ounce) can Eagle® Brand Sweetened Condensed Milk (NOT evaporated milk)
4 teaspoons vanilla extract
2 cups (1 pint) Borden® Whipping Cream, whipped (*do not use non-dairy whipped topping*)

In large bowl, combine sweetened condensed milk and vanilla. Fold in whipped cream. Pour into 9×5-inch loaf pan or other 2-quart container; cover. Freeze 6 hours or until firm. Return leftovers to freezer.

Vanilla Nut: Add ¾ cup chopped nuts. Proceed as above.

Coffee: Dissolve 1 tablespoon instant coffee in 1 teaspoon hot water; add to ice cream mixture. Proceed as above.

Chocolate Chip: Add ½ cup mini chocolate chips. Proceed as above.

MUD PIE

Makes one 9-inch pie

1 (14-ounce) can Eagle® Brand Sweetened Condensed Milk (NOT evaporated milk)
4 teaspoons vanilla extract
1 cup coarsely crushed creme-filled chocolate sandwich cookies (12 cookies)
2 cups (1 pint) Borden® Whipping Cream, whipped (*do not use non-dairy whipped topping*)
1 (9-inch) chocolate crumb crust Chocolate fudge ice cream topping *or* chocolate-flavored syrup Chopped nuts

In large bowl, combine sweetened condensed milk and vanilla. Fold in cookies and whipped cream. Pour into 9×5-inch loaf pan or other 2-quart container; cover. Freeze 6 hours or until firm. Scoop ice cream into prepared crust. Drizzle with topping. Garnish with nuts. Return leftovers to freezer.

MUD PIE

ICE CREAM-MAKER PEACH ICE CREAM

ICE CREAM-MAKER VANILLA ICE CREAM

Makes about 1½ quarts

4 cups (1 quart) Borden® Half-and-Half
1 (14-ounce) can Eagle® Brand Sweetened Condensed Milk (NOT evaporated milk)
1 tablespoon vanilla extract

In large bowl, combine ingredients; mix well. Pour into ice cream freezer container. Freeze according to manufacturer's instructions. Return leftovers to freezer.

Fruit Ice Cream: Reduce half-and-half to 3 cups. Add 1 cup pureed or mashed fruit (bananas, peaches, strawberries, etc.) and few drops food coloring if desired. Proceed as above.

FROZEN ORANGE CREAM

Makes about 1 quart

2 cups (1 pint) Borden® Coffee Cream
1 (14-ounce) can Eagle® Brand Sweetened Condensed Milk (NOT evaporated milk)
1 (6-ounce) can frozen orange juice concentrate, thawed
1 cup cold water
1 teaspoon grated orange rind

In large bowl, combine ingredients; mix well. Pour into 8-inch square pan; cover. Freeze 4 hours or until firm. Remove from freezer 5 minutes before serving. Cut into squares to serve. Return leftovers to freezer.

Frozen Lemon Cream: Omit orange juice concentrate and orange rind. Use ½ cup ReaLemon® Lemon Juice from Concentrate and 1 teaspoon grated lemon rind. Proceed as above.

FROZEN MOCHA CHEESECAKE

Makes one 8- or 9-inch cheesecake

1¼ cups chocolate wafer cookie crumbs
   (about 24 wafers)
¼ cup margarine or butter, melted
¼ cup sugar
1 (8-ounce) package cream cheese,
   softened
1 (14-ounce) can Eagle® Brand
   Sweetened Condensed Milk
   (NOT evaporated milk)
⅔ cup chocolate-flavored syrup
1 to 2 tablespoons instant coffee
1 teaspoon hot water
1 cup (½ pint) Borden® Whipping
   Cream, whipped
   Additional chocolate crumbs,
   optional

Combine crumbs, margarine and sugar; press firmly on bottom and up side of 8- or 9-inch springform pan *or* 13×9-inch baking pan. In large mixer bowl, beat cheese until fluffy. Gradually beat in sweetened condensed milk and syrup until smooth. Dissolve coffee in water; add to cheese mixture. Mix well. Fold in whipped cream. Pour into prepared pan; cover. Freeze 6 hours or overnight. Garnish with additional chocolate crumbs if desired. Return leftovers to freezer.

FROZEN PIÑA COLADA PARFAITS

Makes 6 to 8 servings

1 (14-ounce) can Eagle® Brand Sweetened Condensed Milk (NOT evaporated milk)
½ cup Coco Lopez® Cream of Coconut
⅓ cup pineapple juice
¼ to ⅓ cup dark rum
1 cup (½ pint) Borden® Whipping Cream, whipped (*do not use non-dairy whipped topping*)

In large bowl, combine sweetened condensed milk, cream of coconut, juice and rum. Fold in whipped cream. Spoon equal portions into 6 to 8 individual serving dishes. Freeze 3 hours or until firm. Garnish as desired. Return leftovers to freezer.

FROZEN GRASSHOPPER PARFAITS

Makes 6 to 8 servings

1 (14-ounce) can Eagle® Brand Sweetened Condensed Milk (NOT evaporated milk)
⅓ cup green creme de menthe
⅓ cup white creme de cacao
2 cups (1 pint) Borden® Whipping Cream, whipped (*do not use non-dairy whipped topping*)

In large bowl, combine sweetened condensed milk and liqueurs. Fold in whipped cream. Spoon equal portions into 6 to 8 individual serving dishes. Freeze 3 hours or until firm. Garnish as desired. Return leftovers to freezer.

FROZEN AMARETTO PARFAITS

Makes 6 to 8 servings

1 (14-ounce) can Eagle® Brand Sweetened Condensed Milk (NOT evaporated milk)
⅓ cup amaretto liqueur
1 cup (½ pint) Borden® Whipping Cream, whipped (*do not use non-dairy whipped topping*)

In large bowl, combine sweetened condensed milk and liqueur. Fold in whipped cream. Spoon equal portions into 6 to 8 individual serving dishes. Freeze 3 hours or until firm. Garnish as desired. Return leftovers to freezer.

Frozen Coffee Parfaits: Omit amaretto. Add ⅓ cup coffee-flavored liqueur. Proceed as above.

CLOCKWISE FROM LEFT TO RIGHT: FROZEN GRASSHOPPER PARFAIT, FROZEN PIÑA COLADA PARFAIT, FROZEN AMARETTO PARFAIT

FROZEN PEPPERMINT CHEESECAKE

Makes one 9-inch cheesecake

1¼ cups chocolate wafer cookie crumbs (about 24 wafers)
¼ cup sugar
¼ cup margarine or butter, melted
1 (8-ounce) package cream cheese, softened
1 (14-ounce) can Eagle® Brand Sweetened Condensed Milk (NOT evaporated milk)
1 cup crushed hard peppermint candy Red food coloring, optional
2 cups (1 pint) Borden® Whipping Cream, whipped

Combine crumbs, sugar and margarine; press firmly on bottom and halfway up side of 9-inch springform pan. In large mixer bowl, beat cheese until fluffy. Gradually beat in sweetened condensed milk until smooth. Stir in crushed candy and food coloring if desired. Fold in whipped cream. Pour into prepared pan; cover. Freeze 6 hours or until firm. Garnish as desired. Return leftovers to freezer.

RED, WHITE & BLUEBERRY DELIGHT

Makes 8 to 10 servings

1½ cups graham cracker crumbs
¼ cup sugar
6 tablespoons margarine or butter, melted
1 (14-ounce) can Eagle® Brand Sweetened Condensed Milk (NOT evaporated milk)
⅓ cup ReaLemon® Lemon Juice from Concentrate
2 (8-ounce) containers Borden® Lite-line® Plain Yogurt
2 cups Campfire® Miniature Marshmallows
½ cup chopped pecans
1 pint fresh strawberries, hulled and sliced
1 cup fresh blueberries

Combine crumbs, sugar and margarine. Press on bottom of 12 × 7-inch baking dish. In large bowl, combine sweetened condensed milk, ReaLemon® brand, yogurt, marshmallows and nuts. Spread half the mixture over crust. Top with half the berries, remaining yogurt mixture, then remaining berries. Cover; freeze 6 hours or until firm. Remove from freezer 10 minutes before serving. Return leftovers to freezer.

FROZEN CHOCOLATE BANANA LOAF ▶

Makes 8 to 10 servings

1½ cups chocolate wafer cookie crumbs (about 30 wafers)
¼ cup sugar
3 tablespoons margarine or butter, melted
1 (14-ounce) can Eagle® Brand Sweetened Condensed Milk (NOT evaporated milk)
⅔ cup chocolate-flavored syrup
2 small ripe bananas, mashed (¾ cup)
2 cups (1 pint) Borden® Whipping Cream, whipped (*do not use non-dairy whipped topping*)

Line 9 × 5-inch loaf pan with aluminum foil, extending foil above sides of pan; butter foil. Combine crumbs, sugar and margarine; press firmly on bottom and halfway up sides of prepared pan. In large bowl, combine sweetened condensed milk, syrup and bananas; mix well. Fold in whipped cream. Pour into prepared pan; cover. Freeze 6 hours or until firm. To serve, remove from pan; peel off foil. Garnish as desired. Slice to serve. Return leftovers to freezer.

FROZEN PEANUT BUTTER PIE

Makes one 9- or 10-inch pie

Chocolate Crunch Crust
1 (8-ounce) package cream cheese, softened
1 (14-ounce) can Eagle® Brand Sweetened Condensed Milk (NOT evaporated milk)
¾ cup peanut butter
2 tablespoons ReaLemon® Lemon Juice from Concentrate
1 teaspoon vanilla extract
1 cup (½ pint) Borden® Whipping Cream, whipped, *or* 1 (4-ounce) container frozen non-dairy whipped topping, thawed
Chocolate fudge ice cream topping

Prepare Chocolate Crunch Crust; chill. In large mixer bowl, beat cheese until fluffy. Gradually beat in sweetened condensed milk, then peanut butter until smooth. Stir in ReaLemon® brand and vanilla. Fold in whipped cream. Turn into prepared crust. Drizzle fudge topping over pie. Freeze 4 hours or until firm. Return leftovers to freezer.

Chocolate Crunch Crust: In heavy saucepan, over low heat, melt ⅓ cup margarine or butter and 1 (6-ounce) package semi-sweet chocolate chips. Remove from heat; gently stir in 2½ cups oven-toasted rice cereal until completely coated. Press on bottom and up side to rim of buttered 9- or 10-inch pie plate. Chill 30 minutes.

FROZEN PIÑA COLADA TORTE

Makes 12 servings

1 (7-ounce) package flaked coconut, toasted (2⅔ cups)
3 tablespoons margarine or butter, melted
1 (14-ounce) can Eagle® Brand Sweetened Condensed Milk (NOT evaporated milk)
½ cup Coco Lopez® Cream of Coconut
1 (20-ounce) can crushed pineapple, well drained
2 cups (1 pint) Borden® Whipping Cream, whipped
Maraschino cherries

Reserving ¾ *cup* coconut, combine remaining coconut and margarine; press firmly on bottom of 9-inch springform pan, 13×9-inch baking pan *or* 9-inch square pan. Chill. In large bowl, combine sweetened condensed milk and cream of coconut; stir in *1 cup* pineapple. Fold in whipped cream. Pour half the mixture into prepared pan. Sprinkle with ½ *cup* reserved coconut; top with remaining cream mixture. Freeze 6 hours or until firm. Just before serving, garnish with remaining coconut, remaining pineapple and cherries. Return leftovers to freezer.

FROZEN LEMON SQUARES

Makes 9 servings

1¼ cups graham cracker crumbs
¼ cup sugar
¼ cup margarine or butter, melted
1 (14-ounce) can Eagle® Brand Sweetened Condensed Milk (NOT evaporated milk)
½ cup ReaLemon® Lemon Juice from Concentrate
Few drops yellow food coloring, optional
Whipped topping or whipped cream

Preheat oven to 350°. Combine crumbs, sugar and margarine; press firmly on bottom of 8- or 9-inch square pan. In medium bowl, stir together sweetened condensed milk, ReaLemon® brand and food coloring if desired. Pour into prepared pan. Bake 8 minutes. Cool. Top with whipped topping. Freeze 4 hours or until firm. Let stand 10 minutes before serving. Garnish as desired. Return leftovers to freezer.

Tip: Dessert can be chilled instead of frozen.

FROZEN LEMON SQUARE

CHOCO-CHERRY ICE CREAM LOAF

Makes 8 to 10 servings

2 cups finely crushed creme-filled chocolate sandwich cookies (about 20 cookies)
3 tablespoons margarine or butter, melted
1 (14-ounce) can Eagle® Brand Sweetened Condensed Milk (NOT evaporated milk)
⅔ cup chocolate-flavored syrup
1 (16-ounce) can dark sweet pitted cherries, *well drained* and coarsely chopped
¾ cup chopped nuts
½ to 1 teaspoon almond extract
2 cups (1 pint) Borden® Whipping Cream, whipped (*do not use non-dairy whipped topping*)

Line 9×5-inch loaf pan with aluminum foil, extending foil above sides of pan. Combine crumbs and margarine; press firmly on bottom and halfway up sides of prepared pan. In large bowl, combine sweetened condensed milk and syrup. Stir in cherries, nuts and extract. Fold in whipped cream. Pour into prepared pan. Cover; freeze 6 hours or overnight. To serve, remove from pan; peel off foil and slice. Garnish as desired. Return leftovers to freezer.

Brandied Choco-Cherry Ice Cream Loaf: Omit nuts; soak cherries in ¼ cup brandy 10 minutes. Add to sweetened condensed milk mixture. Proceed as above.

BROWNIE MINT CHOCOLATE CHIP SUNDAE

Makes 10 to 12 servings

1 (21½-ounce) package fudge brownie mix
1 (14-ounce) can Eagle® Brand Sweetened Condensed Milk (NOT evaporated milk)
2 teaspoons peppermint extract
4 to 6 drops green food coloring, optional
2 cups (1 pint) Borden® Whipping Cream, whipped
½ cup mini chocolate chips
    Hot fudge sauce or chocolate-flavored syrup

Prepare brownie mix as package directs. Turn into aluminum foil-lined and greased 13×9-inch baking pan. Bake as directed. Cool completely. In large bowl, combine sweetened condensed milk, extract and food coloring if desired. Fold in whipped cream and chips. Pour over cooled brownie layer. Cover; freeze 6 hours or until firm. To serve, lift from pan with foil; cut into squares. Serve with hot fudge sauce. Return leftovers to freezer.

CHOCOLATE CHIP ICE CREAM SANDWICHES ▲

Makes 12 to 15 servings

1 (14-ounce) can Eagle® Brand
   Sweetened Condensed Milk
   (NOT evaporated milk)
4 teaspoons vanilla extract
2 cups (1 pint) Borden® Whipping
   Cream, whipped (*do not use
   non-dairy whipped topping*)
¾ cup mini chocolate chips
24 to 30 chocolate chip or chocolate
   wafer cookies

In large bowl, combine sweetened
condensed milk and vanilla. Fold in
whipped cream and chips. Pour into
9 × 5-inch loaf pan or other 2-quart
container; cover. Freeze 6 hours or until
firm. Scoop about ¼ cup ice cream onto
bottom of 1 cookie; top with another
cookie, top side up. Press gently. Wrap
tightly in plastic wrap. Repeat for
remaining sandwiches. Store in freezer.

FROZEN CHOCOLATE MOUSSE PIE

Makes one 9-inch pie

2 cups finely crushed creme-filled
   chocolate sandwich cookies
   (about 20 cookies)
¼ cup margarine or butter, melted
1 (6-ounce) package semi-sweet
   chocolate chips *or* 4 (1-ounce)
   squares semi-sweet chocolate,
   melted
1 (14-ounce) can Eagle® Brand
   Sweetened Condensed Milk
   (NOT evaporated milk)
1½ teaspoons vanilla extract
1 cup (½ pint) Borden® Whipping
   Cream, stiffly whipped

Combine crumbs and margarine; press
on bottom and up side to rim of lightly
buttered 9-inch pie plate. Chill. In large
mixer bowl, beat melted chocolate with
sweetened condensed milk and vanilla
until well blended. Chill thoroughly, 10
to 15 minutes. Fold in whipped cream.
Pour into crust. Freeze 6 hours or until
firm. Garnish as desired. Return
leftovers to freezer.

FUDGY ICE CREAM SQUARES

Makes 10 to 12 servings

1½ cups finely crushed creme-filled chocolate sandwich cookies (about 18 cookies)
2 to 3 tablespoons margarine or butter, melted
3 (1-ounce) squares unsweetened chocolate, melted
1 (14-ounce) can Eagle® Brand Sweetened Condensed Milk (NOT evaporated milk)
2 teaspoons vanilla extract
1 cup chopped nuts, optional
2 cups (1 pint) Borden® Whipping Cream, whipped
Whipped topping

Combine crumbs and margarine; press firmly on bottom of 13 × 9-inch baking pan. In large mixer bowl, beat melted chocolate with sweetened condensed milk and vanilla until well blended. Stir in nuts if desired. Fold in whipped cream. Pour into prepared pan. Top with whipped topping. Cover; freeze 6 hours or until firm. Garnish as desired. Return leftovers to freezer.

FUDGY ICE CREAM SQUARE

FROZEN CRANBERRY CHEESE PIE

Makes one 9-inch pie

1½ cups vanilla wafer crumbs (about 40 wafers)
6 tablespoons margarine or butter, melted
2 (3-ounce) packages cream cheese, softened
1 (14-ounce) can Eagle® Brand Sweetened Condensed Milk (NOT evaporated milk)
⅓ cup ReaLemon® Lemon Juice from Concentrate
1 teaspoon vanilla extract
1 (16-ounce) can whole berry cranberry sauce, chilled
Whipped cream, optional

Combine crumbs and margarine; press firmly on bottom and up side to rim of 9-inch pie plate. Chill. Meanwhile, in large mixer bowl, beat cheese until fluffy. Gradually beat in sweetened condensed milk until smooth. Stir in ReaLemon® brand and vanilla. Reserving ½ cup cranberry sauce, add remainder to cheese mixture. Pour into prepared crust. Cover; freeze 6 hours or until firm. Just before serving, garnish with reserved cranberry sauce and whipped cream if desired. Return leftovers to freezer.

FROZEN STRAWBERRY MARGARITA PIE

Makes one 9-inch pie

1¼ cups *finely* crushed pretzel crumbs
¼ cup sugar
½ cup plus 2 tablespoons margarine
  or butter, melted
1 (14-ounce) can Eagle® Brand
  Sweetened Condensed Milk
  (NOT evaporated milk)
1 cup chopped fresh or thawed frozen
  unsweetened strawberries
¼ cup ReaLime® Lime Juice from
  Concentrate
3 to 4 tablespoons tequila
2 tablespoons triple sec or other
  orange-flavored liqueur
2 to 4 drops red food coloring,
  optional
1 cup (½ pint) Borden® Whipping
  Cream, whipped

Combine crumbs, sugar and margarine; press firmly on bottom and up side to rim of lightly buttered 9-inch pie plate. In large bowl, combine sweetened condensed milk, chopped strawberries, ReaLime® brand, tequila, triple sec and food coloring if desired; mix well. Fold in whipped cream. Pour into prepared crust. Freeze 4 hours or until firm. Let stand 10 minutes before serving. Garnish as desired. Return leftovers to freezer.

Margarita Pie: Omit strawberries and red food coloring. Increase ReaLime® brand to ⅓ cup. Proceed as above. Freeze 4 hours or chill 2 hours. Garnish as desired. Return leftovers to freezer or refrigerator.

◀ TORTONI

Makes 1½ to 2 dozen

1 (14-ounce) can Eagle® Brand Sweetened Condensed Milk (NOT evaporated milk)
¼ cup light rum
2 teaspoons vanilla extract
⅔ cup coconut macaroon crumbs (about 5 macaroons)
½ to ¾ cup slivered almonds, toasted
⅓ to ½ cup chopped maraschino cherries
2 cups (1 pint) Borden® Whipping Cream, whipped

In large bowl, combine all ingredients except whipped cream; mix well. Fold in whipped cream. Fill 2½-inch foil cups; cover. Freeze 6 hours or until firm. Garnish as desired. Return leftovers to freezer.

FROZEN MINT CHOCOLATE MOUSSE

Makes 6 to 8 servings

1 (14-ounce) can Eagle® Brand Sweetened Condensed Milk (NOT evaporated milk)
⅔ cup chocolate-flavored syrup
¾ teaspoon peppermint extract
1 cup (½ pint) Borden® Whipping Cream, whipped (*do not use non-dairy whipped topping*)

In large bowl, combine sweetened condensed milk, syrup and extract. Fold in whipped cream. Spoon equal portions into 6 or 8 individual serving dishes. Freeze 3 to 4 hours or until firm. Garnish as desired. Return leftovers to freezer.

CHOCOLATE ICE CREAM CUPS

Makes about 1½ dozen

1 (12-ounce) package semi-sweet chocolate chips
1 (14-ounce) can Eagle® Brand Sweetened Condensed Milk (NOT evaporated milk)
1 cup finely ground pecans
1 teaspoon vanilla extract
   Borden® Ice Cream or Sherbet, any flavor

Use spoon to spread chocolate mixture to form cup.

In small saucepan, over low heat, melt chips with sweetened condensed milk; remove from heat. Stir in pecans and vanilla. Line 2½-inch muffin cups with foil liners. With spoon, spread about 2 tablespoons chocolate mixture on bottom and up side to rim of each cup. Freeze 2 hours or until firm. Before serving, remove foil liners. Fill with ice cream or sherbet. Store unfilled cups tightly covered in freezer.

MICROWAVE: In 1-quart glass measure, combine chips with sweetened condensed milk. Cook on 100% power (high) 3 minutes. Stir until chips melt and mixture is smooth. Stir in pecans and vanilla. Proceed as above.

Chocolate Cup with Creamy Soda Freeze.

SPIRITED MOCHA MOUSSE

Makes 10 to 12 servings

1 tablespoon instant coffee
1 teaspoon hot water
1 (6-ounce) package semi-sweet chocolate chips
1 (14-ounce) can Eagle® Brand Sweetened Condensed Milk (NOT evaporated milk)
¼ cup coffee-flavored liqueur, optional
2 cups (1 pint) Borden® Whipping Cream, whipped (*do not use non-dairy whipped topping*)

In small bowl, dissolve coffee in water; set aside. In medium saucepan, melt chips; remove from heat. Stir in sweetened condensed milk, coffee liquid and liqueur; mix well. Fold in whipped cream. Spoon about ½ cup mixture into individual dessert dishes; cover. Freeze 2 hours or until firm. Garnish as desired. Return leftovers to freezer.

Ice Cream & Frozen Desserts 169

Pour ice cream mixture into aluminum foil-lined round bowl.

Invert ice cream layer on brownie layer; peel off foil.

Spread meringue completely over ice cream and brownie, sealing carefully to edge of brownie.

◄ GRASSHOPPER BAKED ALASKA

Makes 12 to 15 servings

ICE CREAM
1 (14-ounce) can Eagle® Brand Sweetened Condensed Milk (NOT evaporated milk)
⅓ cup green creme de menthe
¼ cup white creme de cacao
2 cups (1 pint) Borden® Whipping Cream, whipped (*do not use non-dairy whipped topping*)
½ cup mini chocolate chips

BROWNIE
1 (15- or 15½-ounce) package brownie mix

MERINGUE
4 egg whites*
¼ teaspoon cream of tartar
½ cup sugar
1 tablespoon unsweetened cocoa

3 to 10 days ahead
1. To prepare ice cream, in large bowl, combine sweetened condensed milk and liqueurs; mix well. Fold in whipped cream and chips. Pour into aluminum foil-lined 2- or 3-quart round mixing bowl. Cover; freeze 8 to 12 hours or until firm.

1 to 5 days ahead
2. Prepare brownie mix as package directs. Pour into greased 8-inch round layer cake pan; bake according to package directions. Remove from pan; cool thoroughly.

1 to 5 days ahead
3. Preheat oven to 500°. In large mixer bowl, beat egg whites and cream of tartar until soft peaks form. Mix sugar and cocoa; gradually beat into egg whites until stiff but not dry. Place prepared brownie layer on ovenproof plate, wooden board or baking sheet. Remove ice cream from bowl; invert onto brownie layer. Trim to fit if desired. Quickly spread meringue over ice cream and brownie, sealing carefully to bottom edge of brownie. Bake 2 to 3 minutes or until lightly browned. Return to freezer; freeze at least 6 hours before serving. Garnish as desired. Return leftovers to freezer.

*Use only Grade A clean, uncracked eggs.

LEMON DESSERT FREEZE

Makes 9 servings

1 cup graham cracker crumbs
3 tablespoons margarine or butter, melted
1 (21- or 22-ounce) can lemon pie filling
1 (14-ounce) can Eagle® Brand Sweetened Condensed Milk (NOT evaporated milk)
½ cup ReaLemon® Lemon Juice from Concentrate
1½ cups frozen non-dairy whipped topping, thawed

Combine crumbs and margarine. Reserving 1 tablespoon crumbs for garnish, press remainder firmly on bottom of 8- or 9-inch square pan. In medium bowl, combine pie filling, sweetened condensed milk and ReaLemon® brand; stir until smooth. Spread into prepared pan. Top with whipped topping; garnish with reserved crumbs. Freeze 4 hours or until firm. Cut into squares to serve. Return leftovers to freezer.

FUDGY CHOCOLATE ICE CREAM

Makes about 1½ quarts

5 (1-ounce) squares unsweetened chocolate, melted
1 (14-ounce) can Eagle® Brand Sweetened Condensed Milk (NOT evaporated milk)
2 teaspoons vanilla extract
2 cups (1 pint) Borden® Half-and-Half
2 cups (1 pint) Borden® Whipping Cream, *unwhipped*
½ cup chopped nuts, optional

In large mixer bowl, beat chocolate, sweetened condensed milk and vanilla. Stir in half-and-half, whipping cream and nuts if desired. Pour into ice cream freezer container. Freeze according to manufacturer's instructions. Return leftovers to freezer.

Refrigerator-Freezer Method: Omit half-and-half. Reduce chocolate to 3 (1-ounce) squares. Whip whipping cream. In large mixer bowl, beat chocolate, sweetened condensed milk and vanilla; fold in whipped cream and nuts if desired. Pour into 9×5-inch loaf pan or other 2-quart container; cover. Freeze 6 hours or until firm. Return leftovers to freezer.

FROZEN PEACH AMARETTO CHEESECAKE

Makes 10 to 12 servings

- 1 cup graham cracker crumbs
- ¼ cup slivered almonds, toasted and finely chopped
- 2 tablespoons sugar
- ⅓ cup margarine or butter, melted
- 1 (8-ounce) package cream cheese, softened
- 1 (14-ounce) can Eagle® Brand Sweetened Condensed Milk (NOT evaporated milk)
- 2 cups pureed fresh or thawed frozen peaches
- ⅓ cup amaretto liqueur
- 1 cup (½ pint) Borden® Whipping Cream, whipped
  Fresh peach slices, optional

Combine crumbs, almonds, sugar and margarine. Press firmly on bottom of 9-inch springform pan. In large mixer bowl, beat cheese until fluffy. Gradually beat in sweetened condensed milk until smooth. Stir in pureed peaches and liqueur. Fold in whipped cream. Pour into prepared pan. Cover; freeze 6 hours or until firm. Remove from freezer 5 minutes before serving. Garnish with peach slices if desired. Return leftovers to freezer.

CREAMY SODA FREEZE

Makes 2 to 3 quarts

- 2 (14-ounce) cans Eagle® Brand Sweetened Condensed Milk (NOT evaporated milk)
- 1 (2-liter) bottle *or* 5 (12-ounce) cans carbonated beverage, any flavor

In electric ice cream freezer container, combine ingredients; mix well. Freeze according to manufacturer's instructions. Store leftovers in freezer.

Shakes: In blender container, combine one-half (14-ounce) can Eagle® Brand Sweetened Condensed Milk, 1 (12-ounce) can carbonated beverage and 3 cups ice. Blend until smooth. Repeat for additional shakes. Store leftovers in freezer. (Makes 1 or 2 quarts)

Frozen Pops: Combine 1 (14-ounce) can Eagle® Brand Sweetened Condensed Milk with 2 (12-ounce) cans carbonated beverage; mix well. Pour equal portions into 8 (5-ounce) paper cold-drink cups. Cover each cup with aluminum foil; make small hole in center of each. Insert a wooden stick into each cup. Freeze 6 hours or until firm. (Makes 8 servings)

CREAMY SODA FREEZE

FROZEN FLUFFY STRAWBERRY PIE

Makes one 9-inch pie

2½ cups flaked coconut, toasted
⅓ cup margarine or butter, melted
1 (3-ounce) package cream cheese, softened
1 (14-ounce) can Eagle® Brand Sweetened Condensed Milk (NOT evaporated milk)
2½ cups fresh or thawed frozen unsweetened strawberries, mashed or pureed (about 1½ cups)
3 tablespoons ReaLemon® Lemon Juice from Concentrate
1 cup (½ pint) Borden® Whipping Cream, whipped
Additional fresh strawberries, optional

Combine coconut and margarine; press firmly on bottom and up side to rim of 9-inch pie plate. In large mixer bowl, beat cheese until fluffy. Gradually beat in sweetened condensed milk until smooth. Stir in pureed strawberries and ReaLemon® brand. Fold in whipped cream. Pour into prepared crust (mixture should mound slightly). Freeze 4 hours or until firm. Before serving, garnish with fresh strawberries if desired. Return leftovers to freezer.

Tip: 1 (9-inch) baked pastry shell can be substituted for coconut crust.

EASY CHOCOLATE ICE CREAM 'N' CAKE

Makes 12 servings

1 (18¼- or 18½-ounce) package white cake mix
1 (14-ounce) can Eagle® Brand Sweetened Condensed Milk (NOT evaporated milk)
⅔ cup chocolate-flavored syrup
1 cup slivered almonds, toasted and chopped, optional
2 cups (1 pint) Borden® Whipping Cream, whipped (*do not use non-dairy whipped topping*)
1 (8-ounce) container frozen non-dairy whipped topping, thawed
Additional chocolate-flavored syrup

Prepare and bake cake mix as directed for 13×9-inch cake. Cool slightly. Turn out onto aluminum foil-covered baking sheet. Cool thoroughly; set aside. In large bowl, combine sweetened condensed milk, ⅔ *cup* syrup and chopped almonds. Fold in whipped cream. Line 13×9-inch baking pan with aluminum foil, extending foil above sides of pan. Pour chocolate mixture into prepared pan; cover. Freeze 6 hours or until firm. Lift ice cream out of pan with foil; turn out evenly on top of cake layer. Trim ice cream to fit cake layer. Quickly frost top and sides with whipped topping. Drizzle with syrup. Return to freezer for at least 2 hours before serving. Return leftovers to freezer.

Tip: Can be made up to 2 weeks ahead. Cover tightly and store in freezer.

FRESH BERRY ICE CREAM

Makes about 1½ quarts

- 3 cups (1½ pints) Borden® Half-and-Half
- 1 (14-ounce) can Eagle® Brand Sweetened Condensed Milk (NOT evaporated milk)
- 2 cups fresh or frozen unsweetened raspberries, strawberries or other berries, mashed or pureed (about 1 cup)
- Few drops red food coloring, optional
- 1 tablespoon vanilla extract

In large bowl, combine ingredients; mix well. Pour into ice cream freezer container. Freeze according to manufacturer's instructions. Return leftovers to freezer.

FROZEN AMARETTO ORANGE BLOSSOM PIE

Makes one 9-inch pie

- 1 (9-inch) baked pastry shell
- 1 (14-ounce) can Eagle® Brand Sweetened Condensed Milk (NOT evaporated milk)
- ½ cup orange carbonated beverage
- 2 tablespoons almond-flavored liqueur
- 1 teaspoon grated orange rind
- Few drops red and yellow food coloring, optional
- 1 (8-ounce) container frozen non-dairy whipped topping, thawed

In large bowl, combine all ingredients except pastry shell and whipped topping; mix well. Fold in whipped topping. Turn into prepared pastry shell. Freeze 4 hours or until set. Garnish as desired. Refrigerate leftovers.

FRESH BERRY ICE CREAM

BLUEBERRY ICE CREAM MERINGUE SQUARES

Makes 10 to 12 servings

1¼ cups graham cracker crumbs
¾ cup sugar
⅓ cup margarine or butter, melted
1 cup fresh *or* dry-pack frozen blueberries, thawed, rinsed and well drained
1 (14-ounce) can Eagle® Brand Sweetened Condensed Milk (NOT evaporated milk)
1 tablespoon grated lemon rind
2 cups (1 pint) Borden® Whipping Cream, whipped (*do not use non-dairy whipped topping*)
4 egg whites*
¼ teaspoon cream of tartar

Combine crumbs, ¼ *cup* sugar and margarine. Press firmly on bottom of 12×7-inch baking dish. In blender container, blend blueberries until smooth. In large bowl, combine blueberries, sweetened condensed milk and rind. Fold in whipped cream. Pour into prepared pan. Cover. Freeze 6 hours or overnight. In small mixer bowl, beat egg whites and cream of tartar until soft peaks form. Gradually beat in remaining ½ *cup* sugar until stiff but not dry. Spread meringue over blueberry ice cream, sealing carefully to edge of dish. Bake in preheated 450° oven 2 minutes or until lightly browned. Return to freezer at least 3 hours before serving. Return leftovers to freezer.

*Use only Grade A clean, uncracked eggs.

FROZEN PEACH CREAM PIES

Makes 2 pies

1 (8-ounce) package cream cheese, softened
1 (14-ounce) can Eagle® Brand Sweetened Condensed Milk (NOT evaporated milk)
1½ cups pureed fresh or thawed frozen peaches
1 tablespoon ReaLemon® Lemon Juice from Concentrate
¼ teaspoon almond extract
Few drops yellow and red food coloring, optional
1 (8-ounce) container frozen non-dairy whipped topping, thawed
2 (6-ounce) packaged graham cracker crumb pie crusts
Fresh peach slices

In large mixer bowl, beat cheese until fluffy. Gradually beat in sweetened condensed milk, then pureed peaches, ReaLemon® brand, extract and food coloring if desired. Fold in whipped topping. Pour equal portions into crusts. Freeze 4 hours or until firm. Remove from freezer 5 minutes before serving. Garnish with peach slices. Return leftovers to freezer.

FROZEN PUDDING-ON-A-STICK

Makes 8 servings

1 (14-ounce) can Eagle® Brand
   Sweetened Condensed Milk
   (NOT evaporated milk)
1½ cups cold water
1 (4-serving size) package *instant*
   pudding mix, any flavor
8 (5-ounce) paper cold-drink cups
8 wooden sticks

In large bowl, combine sweetened
condensed milk and water; mix well.
Add pudding mix; beat well. Chill 5
minutes. Pour equal portions into paper
cups. Insert a wooden stick in center of
each pop; freeze 6 hours or until firm.
To serve, remove from freezer; let stand
5 minutes. Peel off paper cup. Return
leftovers to freezer.

Chocolate Peanut Butter: Beat
sweetened condensed milk and ¼ cup
peanut butter until smooth. Gradually
beat in water then chocolate pudding
mix. Proceed as above.

FROZEN PUDDING-ON-A-STICK

FROZEN AMARETTO TORTE

Makes 12 to 15 servings

2 cups chocolate wafer cookie crumbs
   (about 40 wafers)
½ cup slivered almonds, toasted and
   chopped
⅓ cup margarine or butter, melted
1 (6-ounce) package butterscotch-
   flavored chips
1 (14-ounce) can Eagle® Brand
   Sweetened Condensed Milk
   (NOT evaporated milk)
1 (16-ounce) container Borden® Sour
   Cream
⅓ cup amaretto liqueur
1 cup (½ pint) Borden® Whipping
   Cream, whipped

Combine crumbs, almonds and
margarine. Reserving *1½ cups* crumb
mixture, press remainder firmly on
bottom of 9-inch springform pan. In
small saucepan, over medium heat,
melt chips with sweetened condensed
milk. In large bowl, combine sour cream
and amaretto; mix well. Stir in
butterscotch mixture. Fold in whipped
cream. Pour half the amaretto mixture
over prepared crust; top with *1 cup*
reserved crumbs, then remaining
amaretto mixture. Top with remaining
½ cup crumbs; cover. Freeze 6 hours or
until firm. Return leftovers to freezer.

EASY HOMEMADE VANILLA ICE CREAM 'N' COOKIES ▲

Makes about 1½ quarts

1 (14-ounce) can Eagle® Brand Sweetened Condensed Milk (NOT evaporated milk)
4 teaspoons vanilla extract
2 cups (1 pint) Borden® Whipping Cream, whipped (*do not use non-dairy whipped topping*)
1 cup coarsely crushed creme-filled chocolate sandwich cookies (12 cookies)

In large bowl, combine sweetened condensed milk and vanilla. Fold in whipped cream and cookies. Pour into 9×5-inch loaf pan or other 2-quart container; cover. Freeze 6 hours or until firm. Let stand 5 minutes before serving. Return leftovers to freezer.

PINEAPPLE PARFAIT SQUARES

Makes 9 to 12 servings

1 (20-ounce) can crushed pineapple, well drained
1 (16-ounce) container Borden® Sour Cream
1 (14-ounce) can Eagle® Brand Sweetened Condensed Milk (NOT evaporated milk)
¼ cup ReaLemon® Lemon Juice from Concentrate
¾ cup chopped pecans
12 maraschino cherries

In large bowl, combine pineapple, sour cream, sweetened condensed milk and ReaLemon® brand; mix well. Spread into 8-inch square pan; garnish with nuts and cherries. Freeze 3 hours or until firm. Remove from freezer 10 minutes before serving. Cut into squares. Return leftovers to freezer.

Top row: Coconut
Rum Balls (recipe, page 182),
Chocolate Pecan Drops,
Fruit Bon Bons (recipes, page 183),
Milk Chocolate Bourbon Balls
(recipe, page 184)
and Buckeyes (recipe, page 185).
Bottom row: Creamy White
Cherry Fudge (recipe, page 184),
Mint Chocolate Fudge (recipe, page 186),
Peanut Butter Logs (recipe, page 184) and
Foolproof Dark Chocolate Fudge (recipe, page 182).

CANDIES & CONFECTIONS

FOOLPROOF DARK CHOCOLATE FUDGE

Makes about 2 pounds

3 (6-ounce) packages semi-sweet chocolate chips
1 (14-ounce) can Eagle® Brand Sweetened Condensed Milk (NOT evaporated milk)
Dash salt
½ to 1 cup chopped nuts
1½ teaspoons vanilla extract

In heavy saucepan, over low heat, melt chips with sweetened condensed milk and salt. Remove from heat; stir in nuts and vanilla. Spread evenly into waxed paper-lined 8- or 9-inch square pan. Chill 2 hours or until firm. Turn fudge onto cutting board; peel off paper and cut into squares. Store loosely covered at room temperature.

MICROWAVE: In 1-quart glass measure, combine chips with sweetened condensed milk. Cook on 100% power (high) 3 minutes; stir until smooth. Stir in remaining ingredients. Proceed as above.

Creamy Dark Chocolate Fudge: Melt 2 cups Campfire® Miniature Marshmallows with chips and sweetened condensed milk. Proceed as above.

Milk Chocolate Fudge: Omit 1 (6-ounce) package semi-sweet chocolate chips. Add 1 cup milk chocolate chips. Proceed as above.

Creamy Milk Chocolate Fudge: Omit 1 (6-ounce) package semi-sweet chocolate chips. Add 1 cup milk chocolate chips and 2 cups Campfire® Miniature Marshmallows. Proceed as above.

Mexican Chocolate Fudge: Reduce vanilla to 1 teaspoon. Add 1 tablespoon instant coffee and 1 teaspoon ground cinnamon to sweetened condensed milk. Proceed as above.

Butterscotch Fudge: Omit chocolate chips and vanilla. In heavy saucepan, melt 2 (12-ounce) packages butterscotch-flavored chips with sweetened condensed milk. Remove from heat; stir in 2 tablespoons white vinegar, ⅛ teaspoon salt, ½ teaspoon maple flavoring and 1 cup chopped nuts. Proceed as above.

COCONUT RUM BALLS

Makes about 8 dozen

1 (12-ounce) package vanilla wafers, finely crushed (about 3 cups crumbs)
1 (3½-ounce) can flaked coconut (1⅓ cups)
1 cup finely chopped nuts
1 (14-ounce) can Eagle® Brand Sweetened Condensed Milk (NOT evaporated milk)
¼ cup rum
Additional flaked coconut or confectioners' sugar

In large bowl, combine crumbs, coconut and nuts. Add sweetened condensed milk and rum; mix well. Chill 4 hours. Shape into 1-inch balls. Roll in coconut. Store tightly covered in refrigerator.

Tip: Flavor of these candies improves after 24 hours. They can be made ahead and stored in refrigerator for several weeks.

To make Strawberry Bon Bons, form mixture into strawberry shapes; coat with gelatin.

Use pastry bag with open star tip to pipe green frosting onto strawberries to form stems.

FRUIT BON BONS

Makes about 5 dozen

1 (14-ounce) can Eagle® Brand Sweetened Condensed Milk (NOT evaporated milk)
2 (7-ounce) packages flaked coconut (5⅓ cups)
1 (8-serving size) package fruit flavor gelatin, any flavor
1 cup ground blanched almonds
1 teaspoon almond extract
Food coloring, optional

In large bowl, combine sweetened condensed milk, coconut, ⅓ cup gelatin, almonds, extract and enough food coloring to tint mixture desired shade. Chill 1 hour or until firm enough to handle. Using about ½ tablespoon mixture for each, shape into 1-inch balls. Sprinkle remaining gelatin onto waxed paper; roll each ball in gelatin to coat. Place on waxed paper-lined baking sheets; chill. Store covered at room temperature or in refrigerator.

Strawberry Bon Bons: Using strawberry flavor gelatin, prepare bon bon mixture as above. Form into strawberry shapes. In small bowl, combine 2¼ cups sifted confectioners' sugar, 3 tablespoons Borden® Whipping Cream and few drops green food coloring. (Or, use green tube decorator icing). Using pastry bag with open star tip, pipe small amount on top of each strawberry.

CHOCOLATE PECAN DROPS

Makes about 5 dozen

1 (11½-ounce) package milk chocolate chips
1 (6-ounce) package semi-sweet chocolate chips
¼ cup margarine or butter
1 (14-ounce) can Eagle® Brand Sweetened Condensed Milk (NOT evaporated milk)
⅛ teaspoon salt
2 cups coarsely chopped pecans
2 teaspoons vanilla extract
Pecan halves

In heavy saucepan, over medium heat, melt chips and margarine with sweetened condensed milk and salt. Remove from heat; stir in chopped nuts and vanilla. Drop by teaspoonfuls onto waxed paper-lined baking sheets. Top with pecan halves. Chill. Store tightly covered.

MICROWAVE: In 2-quart glass measure, combine chips, margarine, sweetened condensed milk and salt. Cook on 100% power (high) 3 minutes, stirring after 1½ minutes. Stir until smooth. Stir in remaining ingredients. Proceed as above.

Candies & Confections   183

CREAMY WHITE FUDGE

Makes about 2¼ pounds

1½ pounds white confectioners' coating*
1 (14-ounce) can Eagle® Brand Sweetened Condensed Milk (NOT evaporated milk)
⅛ teaspoon salt
¾ to 1 cup chopped nuts
1½ teaspoons vanilla extract

In heavy saucepan, over low heat, melt coating with sweetened condensed milk and salt. Remove from heat; stir in nuts and vanilla. Spread evenly into waxed paper-lined 8- or 9-inch square pan. Chill 2 hours or until firm. Turn fudge onto cutting board; peel off paper and cut into squares. Store tightly covered at room temperature.

MICROWAVE: In 2-quart glass measure, combine coating, sweetened condensed milk and salt. Cook on 100% power (high) 3 to 5 minutes, stirring after 3 minutes. Stir until smooth. Stir in vanilla and nuts. Proceed as above.

Praline Fudge: Omit vanilla. Add 1 teaspoon maple flavoring and 1 cup chopped pecans. Proceed as above.

Confetti Fudge: Omit nuts. Add 1 cup chopped mixed candied fruit. Proceed as above.

Rum Raisin Fudge: Omit vanilla. Add 1½ teaspoons white vinegar, 1 teaspoon rum flavoring and ¾ cup raisins. Proceed as above.

Cherry Fudge: Omit nuts. Add 1 cup chopped candied cherries.

*White confectioners' coating can be purchased in candy specialty stores.

PEANUT BUTTER LOGS

Makes two 12-inch logs

1 (12-ounce) package peanut butter flavored chips
1 (14-ounce) can Eagle® Brand Sweetened Condensed Milk (NOT evaporated milk)
1 cup Campfire® Miniature Marshmallows
1 cup chopped peanuts

In heavy saucepan, over low heat, melt chips with sweetened condensed milk. Add marshmallows; stir until melted. Remove from heat; cool 20 minutes. Divide in half; place each portion on a 20-inch piece of waxed paper. Shape each into a 12-inch log. Roll in peanuts. Wrap tightly; chill 2 hours or until firm. Remove paper; cut into ¼-inch slices.

MICROWAVE: In 2-quart glass measure, combine chips, sweetened condensed milk and marshmallows. Cook on 100% power (high) 4 minutes or until melted, stirring after 2 minutes. Stir until smooth. Let stand at room temperature 1 hour. Proceed as above.

MILK CHOCOLATE BOURBON BALLS

Makes about 5½ dozen

1 (12-ounce) package vanilla wafers, finely crushed (about 3 cups crumbs)
5 tablespoons bourbon or brandy
1 (11½-ounce) package milk chocolate chips
1 (14-ounce) can Eagle® Brand Sweetened Condensed Milk (NOT evaporated milk)
Finely chopped nuts

In medium bowl, combine crumbs and bourbon. In heavy saucepan, over low heat, melt chips. Remove from heat; add sweetened condensed milk. Gradually add crumb mixture; mix well. Let stand at room temperature 30 minutes or chill. Shape into 1-inch balls; roll in nuts. Store tightly covered.

Tip: Flavor of these candies improves after 24 hours. They can be made ahead and stored in refrigerator or freezer.

BUCKEYES

Makes about 7 dozen

2 (3-ounce) packages cream cheese, softened
1 (14-ounce) can Eagle® Brand Sweetened Condensed Milk (NOT evaporated milk)
2 (12-ounce) packages peanut butter flavored chips
1 cup finely chopped peanuts
½ pound chocolate confectioners' coating*

In large mixer bowl, beat cheese until fluffy. Gradually beat in sweetened condensed milk until smooth. In heavy saucepan, over low heat, melt peanut butter chips; stir into cheese mixture. Add peanuts. Chill 2 to 3 hours; shape into 1-inch balls. In small heavy saucepan, over low heat, melt confectioners' coating. With wooden pick, dip each ball into melted coating, not covering completely. Place on waxed paper-lined baking sheets until firm. Store covered at room temperature or in refrigerator.

*Chocolate confectioners' coating can be purchased in candy specialty stores.

FUDGY COCOA TRUFFLES

Makes about 4 dozen

½ cup margarine or butter
¾ cup unsweetened cocoa
1 (14-ounce) can Eagle® Brand Sweetened Condensed Milk (NOT evaporated milk)
1 teaspoon vanilla extract *or* rum flavoring
Additional unsweetened cocoa

In heavy saucepan, over low heat, melt margarine. Add ¾ *cup* cocoa, then sweetened condensed milk; mix until smooth and well blended. Over medium heat, cook and stir until thickened and smooth, about 5 minutes. Remove from heat; stir in vanilla. Chill 3 hours or until firm. Shape into 1¼-inch balls. Roll in additional cocoa. Chill until firm. Store covered in refrigerator.

MICROWAVE: In 1-quart glass measure, melt margarine on 100% power (high) 1 minute. Add ¾ *cup* cocoa, then sweetened condensed milk; mix until smooth and well blended. Cook on 100% power (high) 2 to 3 minutes or until thickened, stirring after each minute until smooth. Proceed as above.

FUDGY COCOA TRUFFLES

CHOCOLATE CHERRY LOGS

Makes two 12-inch logs

- 3 (6-ounce) packages semi-sweet chocolate chips
- 1 (14-ounce) can Eagle® Brand Sweetened Condensed Milk (NOT evaporated milk)
- 1 (6-ounce) container red or green candied cherries, chopped (about 1 cup)
- 1 teaspoon almond extract
- 1½ cups slivered almonds, toasted and chopped

In heavy saucepan, over low heat, melt chips with sweetened condensed milk. Remove from heat. Stir in cherries and extract. Chill 30 minutes. Divide in half; place each portion on a 20-inch piece of waxed paper. Shape each into a 12-inch log. Roll in nuts. Wrap tightly; chill 2 hours or until firm. Remove paper; cut into ¼-inch slices to serve. Store covered in refrigerator.

MICROWAVE: In 2-quart glass measure, combine chips and sweetened condensed milk. Cook on 100% power (high) 3 minutes, stirring after 1½ minutes. Stir until smooth. Stir in cherries and extract. Chill 1 hour. Proceed as above.

CHOCOLATE CHERRY LOGS

MINT CHOCOLATE FUDGE

Makes about 1¾ pounds

- 1 (12-ounce) package semi-sweet chocolate chips
- 1 (14-ounce) can Eagle® Brand Sweetened Condensed Milk (NOT evaporated milk)
- 2 teaspoons vanilla extract
- 6 ounces white confectioners' coating* *or* 1 cup deluxe white baking pieces
- 1 tablespoon peppermint extract
- 1 drop green or red food coloring, optional

In heavy saucepan, over low heat, melt chips with *1 cup* sweetened condensed milk; add vanilla. Spread *half* the mixture into waxed paper-lined 8- or 9-inch square pan; chill 10 minutes or until firm. Hold remaining chocolate mixture at room temperature. In heavy saucepan, over low heat, melt white confectioners' coating with remaining sweetened condensed milk (mixture will be thick). Add peppermint extract and food coloring if desired. Spread on chilled chocolate layer; chill 10 minutes longer or until firm. Spread reserved chocolate mixture on mint layer. Chill 2 hours or until firm. Turn onto cutting board; peel off paper and cut into squares. Store loosely covered at room temperature.

*Confectioners' coating can be purchased in candy specialty stores.

CHOCOLATE TRUFFLES

Makes about 6 dozen

3 (6-ounce) packages semi-sweet chocolate chips
1 (14-ounce) can Eagle® Brand Sweetened Condensed Milk (NOT evaporated milk)
1 tablespoon vanilla extract
Finely chopped nuts, flaked coconut, chocolate sprinkles, colored sprinkles, unsweetened cocoa *or* colored sugar

In heavy saucepan, over low heat, melt chips with sweetened condensed milk. Remove from heat; stir in vanilla. Chill 2 hours or until firm. Shape into 1-inch balls; roll in any of the above coatings. Chill 1 hour or until firm. Store covered at room temperature.

MICROWAVE: In 1-quart glass measure, combine chips and sweetened condensed milk. Cook on 100% power (high) 3 minutes, stirring after 1½ minutes. Stir until smooth. Proceed as above.

Amaretto: Omit vanilla. Add 3 tablespoons amaretto liqueur and ½ teaspoon almond extract. Roll in finely chopped toasted almonds.

Orange: Omit vanilla. Add 3 tablespoons orange-flavored liqueur. Roll in finely chopped toasted almonds mixed with finely grated orange rind.

Rum: Omit vanilla. Add ¼ cup dark rum. Roll in flaked coconut.

Bourbon: Omit vanilla. Add 3 tablespoons bourbon. Roll in finely chopped toasted nuts.

GOLDEN SNACKING GRANOLA

Makes about 2½ quarts

2 cups oats
1½ cups coarsely chopped nuts
1 (3½-ounce) can flaked coconut
   (1⅓ cups)
½ cup sunflower meats
½ cup wheat germ
2 tablespoons sesame seeds
1 teaspoon ground cinnamon
1 teaspoon salt
1 (14-ounce) can Eagle® Brand
   Sweetened Condensed Milk
   (NOT evaporated milk)
¼ cup vegetable oil
1 cup raisins
1 cup banana chips, optional

Preheat oven to 300°. In large bowl, combine all ingredients except raisins and banana chips; mix well. Spread evenly in aluminum foil-lined 15 × 10-inch jellyroll pan or baking sheet. Bake 55 to 60 minutes, stirring every 15 minutes. Remove from oven; stir in raisins and banana chips if desired. Cool. Store tightly covered at room temperature.

MAPLE CREAM CUPS

Makes about 4 dozen

**1 (14-ounce) can Eagle® Brand
Sweetened Condensed Milk
(NOT evaporated milk)**
**1¼ pounds chocolate confectioners'
coating***
48 (1½-inch) paper or foil candy cups
½ cup chopped nuts
¾ teaspoon maple flavoring

Caramelize sweetened condensed milk in advance. In top of double boiler, over hot water, melt chocolate coating. With small brush, using about 1 teaspoon chocolate, coat bottom and up side to top of candy cups. Sprinkle nuts over bottom of cups. Chill until firm, about 15 minutes. Stir together *caramelized* sweetened condensed milk and maple flavoring. Spoon equal portions into chocolate cups. Brush tops with remaining melted chocolate to cover completely; chill until firm. Store covered at room temperature or in refrigerator.

**TO CARAMELIZE EAGLE® BRAND
SWEETENED CONDENSED MILK**

Oven Method: Preheat oven to 425°. Pour sweetened condensed milk into 8- or 9-inch pie plate. Cover with aluminum foil; place in shallow pan. Fill pan with hot water. Bake 1 to 1½ hours or until thick and light caramel-colored. Remove foil; cool. Chill thoroughly.

Stovetop Method: Pour sweetened condensed milk into top of double boiler; cover. Place over boiling water. Simmer 1 to 1½ hours or until thick and light caramel-colored. Beat until smooth. Cool. Chill thoroughly.

Microwave Method: Pour sweetened condensed milk into 2-quart glass measure. Cook on 50% power (medium) 4 minutes, stirring briskly every 2 minutes until smooth. Cook on 30% power (medium-low) 12 to 18 minutes or until caramel-colored, stirring briskly every 2 minutes until smooth. Cool. Chill thoroughly.

*Confectioners' coating can be purchased in candy specialty stores.

**CAUTION: NEVER HEAT
UNOPENED CAN.**

ROCKY ROAD CANDY

Makes about 3½ dozen

**1 (12-ounce) package semi-sweet
chocolate chips**
2 tablespoons margarine or butter
**1 (14-ounce) can Eagle® Brand
Sweetened Condensed Milk
(NOT evaporated milk)**
2 cups dry-roasted peanuts
**1 (10½-ounce) package Campfire®
Miniature Marshmallows**

In heavy saucepan, over low heat, melt chips and margarine with sweetened condensed milk; remove from heat. In large bowl, combine peanuts and marshmallows; stir in chocolate mixture. Spread in waxed paper-lined 13×9-inch pan. Chill 2 hours or until firm. Remove from pan; peel off paper and cut into squares. Store loosely covered at room temperature.

MICROWAVE: In 1-quart glass measure, combine chips, margarine and sweetened condensed milk. Cook on 100% power (high) 3 minutes, stirring after 1½ minutes. Stir until smooth. Let stand 5 minutes. Proceed as above.

APRICOT ALMOND CHEWIES

Makes about 6½ dozen

4 cups finely chopped dried apricots (about 1 pound)
4 cups flaked coconut *or* coconut macaroon crumbs (about 21 macaroons)
2 cups slivered almonds, toasted and finely chopped
1 (14-ounce) can Eagle® Brand Sweetened Condensed Milk (NOT evaporated milk)

In large bowl, combine ingredients. Chill 2 hours. Shape into 1-inch balls. Store tightly covered in refrigerator.

CHIPPER PEANUT CANDY

Makes about 2 pounds

1 (6-ounce) package semi-sweet chocolate chips *or* butterscotch-flavored chips
1 (14-ounce) can Eagle® Brand Sweetened Condensed Milk (NOT evaporated milk)
1 cup peanut butter
2 cups crushed potato chips
1 cup coarsely chopped peanuts

In large heavy saucepan, over low heat, melt chips with sweetened condensed milk and peanut butter; stir until well blended. Remove from heat. Add potato chips and peanuts; mix well. Press into aluminum foil-lined 8- or 9-inch square pan. Chill 2 hours or until firm. Turn onto cutting board; peel off foil and cut into squares. Store loosely covered at room temperature.

MICROWAVE: In 2-quart glass measure, combine sweetened condensed milk, chocolate chips and peanut butter. Cook on 100% power (high) 4 minutes, stirring after 2 minutes. Stir until smooth. Proceed as above.

CRUNCHY CLUSTERS

Makes about 3 dozen

1 (12-ounce) package semi-sweet chocolate chips *or* 3 (6-ounce) packages butterscotch-flavored chips
1 (14-ounce) can Eagle® Brand Sweetened Condensed Milk (NOT evaporated milk)
1 (3-ounce) can chow mein noodles *or* 2 cups pretzel sticks, broken into ½-inch pieces
1 cup dry-roasted peanuts *or* whole roasted almonds

In heavy saucepan, over low heat, melt chips with sweetened condensed milk. Remove from heat. In large bowl, combine noodles and nuts; stir in chocolate mixture. Drop by tablespoonfuls onto waxed paper-lined baking sheets; chill 2 hours or until firm. Store loosely covered at room temperature.

MICROWAVE: In 2-quart glass measure, combine chips and sweetened condensed milk. Cook on 100% power (high) 3 minutes, stirring after 1½ minutes. Stir until smooth. Proceed as above.

TOP TO BOTTOM: APRICOT ALMOND CHEWIES, CHIPPER PEANUT CANDY, CARAMEL PEANUT BALLS (PAGE 192), CRUNCHY CLUSTERS—BUTTERSCOTCH AND CHOCOLATE, CHIPPER PEANUT CANDY

WHITE TRUFFLES

Makes about 8 dozen

2 pounds white confectioners' coating*
1 (14-ounce) can Eagle® Brand Sweetened Condensed Milk (NOT evaporated milk)
1 tablespoon vanilla extract
1 pound dark chocolate confectioners' coating*, melted, *or* unsweetened cocoa

In heavy saucepan, over low heat, melt white confectioners' coating with sweetened condensed milk. Remove from heat; stir in vanilla. Cool. Shape into 1-inch balls. With wooden pick, partially dip each ball into melted chocolate confectioners' coating or roll in cocoa. Place on waxed paper-lined baking sheets until firm. Store covered at room temperature or in refrigerator.

MICROWAVE: In 2-quart glass measure, combine white confectioners' coating and sweetened condensed milk. Cook on 100% power (high) 3 to 3½ minutes or until coating melts, stirring after 1½ minutes. Stir until smooth. Proceed as above.

*Confectioners' coatings can be purchased in candy specialty stores.

CARAMEL PEANUT BALLS

Makes about 4½ dozen

3 cups *finely* chopped dry-roasted peanuts
1 (14-ounce) can Eagle® Brand Sweetened Condensed Milk (NOT evaporated milk)
1 teaspoon vanilla extract
½ pound chocolate confectioners' coating*

In heavy saucepan, combine peanuts, sweetened condensed milk and vanilla. Over medium heat, cook and stir 8 to 10 minutes or until mixture forms ball around spoon and pulls away from side of pan. Cool 10 minutes. Chill if desired. Shape into 1-inch balls. In small heavy saucepan, over low heat, melt confectioners' coating. With wooden pick, dip each ball into melted coating, not covering completely. Place on waxed paper-lined baking sheets until firm. Store covered at room temperature or in refrigerator.

*Chocolate confectioners' coating can be purchased in candy specialty stores.

WHITE TRUFFLES

MARBLED CHOCOLATE FUDGE

Makes about 2½ pounds

3 (6-ounce) packages semi-sweet
   chocolate chips
1 (14-ounce) can Eagle® Brand
   Sweetened Condensed Milk
   (NOT evaporated milk)
   Dash salt
1½ teaspoons vanilla extract
1 (10-ounce) package deluxe white
   baking pieces, coarsely chopped

In heavy saucepan, over low heat, melt
chips with sweetened condensed milk
and salt. Remove from heat; stir in
vanilla then white baking pieces. Stir
just until blended. Spread evenly into
waxed paper-lined 8- or 9-inch square
pan. Chill 2 hours or until firm. Turn
fudge onto cutting board; peel off paper
and cut into squares. Store loosely
covered at room temperature.

MICROWAVE: In 1-quart glass
measure, combine chips with sweetened
condensed milk. Cook on 100% power
(high) 3 minutes; stir until smooth. Stir
in remaining ingredients. Proceed as
above.

TOASTED VIENNA CHUNKS

Makes about 5 dozen

½ loaf Vienna or French bread, cut
   into 1-inch cubes
1 (14-ounce) can Eagle® Brand
   Sweetened Condensed Milk
   (NOT evaporated milk)
1 (7-ounce) package flaked coconut
   (2⅔ cups)

Preheat oven to 350°. Dip bread into
sweetened condensed milk; allow to
drain briefly. Roll in coconut. Place on
aluminum foil-lined and greased baking
sheets; bake 8 minutes or until coconut
is toasted. *Immediately* remove from
baking sheets. Store loosely covered at
room temperature.

Tip: For a campfire treat, toast chunks
over open fire.

WALNUT RUM FUDGE

Makes about 2½ pounds

1½ pounds white confectioners'
   coating*
1 (14-ounce) can Eagle® Brand
   Sweetened Condensed Milk
   (NOT evaporated milk)
⅛ teaspoon salt
1½ teaspoons white vinegar
1 teaspoon rum flavoring
1 cup chopped walnuts

In large saucepan, over low heat, melt
coating with sweetened condensed milk
and salt. Remove from heat; stir in
remaining ingredients. Spread evenly
into waxed paper-lined 8- or 9-inch
square pan. Chill 2 hours or until firm.
Turn fudge onto cutting board; peel off
paper and cut into squares. Store tightly
covered at room temperature.

*White confectioners' coating can be
purchased in candy specialty stores.

LEFT TO RIGHT: GINGER ORANGE NUT BALLS, EASY PEANUT BUTTER
CHOCOLATE FUDGE, CHOCOLATE FRUIT BALLS AND SCOTCHY CRITTERS

EASY PEANUT BUTTER CHOCOLATE FUDGE

Makes about 2 pounds

1 (12-ounce) package peanut butter
  flavored chips
¼ cup margarine or butter
1 (14-ounce) can Eagle® Brand
  Sweetened Condensed Milk
  (NOT evaporated milk)
½ cup chopped peanuts, optional
1 (6-ounce) package semi-sweet
  chocolate chips

In heavy saucepan, melt peanut butter
chips and 2 *tablespoons* margarine with
1 cup sweetened condensed milk.
Remove from heat; stir in peanuts.
Spread into waxed paper-lined 8-inch
square pan. In small heavy saucepan,
melt chocolate chips and remaining *2
tablespoons* margarine with remaining
sweetened condensed milk. Spread
chocolate mixture on top of peanut
butter mixture. Chill 2 hours or until
firm. Turn fudge onto cutting board;
peel off paper and cut into squares.
Store loosely covered at room
temperature.

GINGER ORANGE NUT BALLS

Makes about 8 dozen

1 (16-ounce) package ginger snap
  cookies, finely crushed (about
  4 cups crumbs)
1 (14-ounce) can Eagle® Brand
  Sweetened Condensed Milk
  (NOT evaporated milk)
1 (3½-ounce) can flaked coconut
  (1⅓ cups)
1 cup finely chopped nuts
1 cup raisins
⅓ cup orange juice
1 tablespoon grated orange rind
  Additional flaked coconut and
  grated orange rind

In large bowl, combine all ingredients
except additional coconut and rind.
Chill at least 1 hour. Shape into 1-inch
balls. Roll in additional coconut mixed
with rind. Store tightly covered in
refrigerator.

Tip: Flavor of these candies improves
after 24 hours. They can be made ahead
and stored in refrigerator for several
weeks.

CHOCOLATE FRUIT BALLS

Makes about 10 dozen

2½ cups vanilla wafer crumbs (about 65 wafers)
1 (14-ounce) can Eagle® Brand Sweetened Condensed Milk (NOT evaporated milk)
1 (8-ounce) package chopped dates
1 cup finely chopped nuts
½ cup chopped candied cherries
2 tablespoons unsweetened cocoa
  Confectioners' sugar *or* unsweetened cocoa
  Additional candied cherries, optional

In large bowl, combine all ingredients except confectioners' sugar and additional cherries; mix well. Chill 1 hour. Shape into 1-inch balls. Roll in confectioners' sugar. Store tightly covered in refrigerator. Garnish with additional candied cherries if desired.

Tip: Flavor of these candies improves after 24 hours. They can be made ahead and stored in refrigerator for several weeks.

SCOTCHY CRITTERS

Makes about 5 dozen

1 (6-ounce) package butterscotch-flavored chips
1 (14-ounce) can Eagle® Brand Sweetened Condensed Milk (NOT evaporated milk)
2 teaspoons white vinegar
4 cups pecan halves (¾ pound)
1 (11½-ounce) package milk chocolate chips
1 teaspoon vanilla extract

In small heavy saucepan, over low heat, melt butterscotch chips with ⅓ *cup* sweetened condensed milk. Remove from heat; stir in vinegar. Drop by half teaspoonfuls onto waxed paper-lined baking sheets. Arrange 3 pecan halves on each butterscotch drop. In large heavy saucepan, over low heat, melt milk chocolate chips with remaining sweetened condensed milk and vanilla. Remove from heat; hold chocolate mixture over hot water. Drop chocolate by heaping teaspoonfuls over pecan clusters. Chill 2 hours or until firm. Store loosely covered.

MICROWAVE: In 1-quart glass measure, combine butterscotch chips and ⅓ *cup* sweetened condensed milk. Cook on 100% power (high) 1½ minutes. Stir to melt chips. Add vinegar. Proceed as above. In 1-quart glass measure, combine milk chocolate chips with remaining sweetened condensed milk. Cook on 100% power (high) 2 minutes. Stir until smooth. Add vanilla. Proceed as above.

Orange Pineapple Punch (recipe, page 198)

ORANGE PINEAPPLE PUNCH

Makes about 4 quarts

1 (14-ounce) can Eagle® Brand
   Sweetened Condensed Milk
   (NOT evaporated milk)
1 (46-ounce) can pineapple juice,
   chilled
1 (6-ounce) can frozen orange juice
   concentrate, thawed
2 (32-ounce) bottles ginger ale,
   chilled
   Borden® Orange Sherbet

In large punch bowl, combine
sweetened condensed milk, pineapple
juice and juice concentrate. Just before
serving, add ginger ale and scoops of
sherbet. Garnish as desired. Refrigerate
leftovers.

SPARKLING APPLE JACK CREAM

Makes about 1¾ quarts

1 (14-ounce) can Eagle® Brand
   Sweetened Condensed Milk
   (NOT evaporated milk)
1 cup apple-flavored liqueur
2 cups (1 pint) Borden® Whipping
   Cream, *unwhipped*
1 (750 mL) bottle sparkling apple
   cider

In blender container, combine all
ingredients except apple cider; blend
until smooth. Just before serving, add
apple cider; stir. Serve over ice.
Refrigerate leftovers.

SPIRITED COFFEE MILK PUNCH

Makes about 1½ quarts

4 cups Borden® Milk
1 (14-ounce) can Eagle® Brand
   Sweetened Condensed Milk
   (NOT evaporated milk)
3 to 4 teaspoons instant coffee
⅓ cup bourbon
⅓ cup coffee-flavored liqueur
1 cup (½ pint) Borden® Whipping
   Cream, whipped
   Dash ground cinnamon
   Dash ground nutmeg

In large mixer bowl, combine milk,
sweetened condensed milk and coffee;
beat on low speed until coffee dissolves.
Stir in bourbon and liqueur; chill. Before
serving, top with whipped cream,
cinnamon and nutmeg. Refrigerate
leftovers.

Holiday Milk Punch: Omit instant
coffee and coffee-flavored liqueur.
Increase bourbon to ½ cup; add 1
teaspoon vanilla extract. Proceed as
above.

MOCHA GROG

Makes about 1½ quarts

⅓ cup unsweetened cocoa
1 teaspoon ground cinnamon
½ teaspoon salt
1 (14-ounce) can Eagle® Brand
   Sweetened Condensed Milk
   (NOT evaporated milk)
4 cups water
1½ cups freshly brewed coffee
½ cup brandy
¼ cup light rum

In large saucepan, combine cocoa,
cinnamon and salt. Add sweetened
condensed milk; mix until smooth. Over
medium heat, slowly stir in water,
coffee, brandy and rum. Heat through,
stirring occasionally. Refrigerate
leftovers.

BANANA SHAKE

Makes about 5 cups

2 ripe bananas, cut up (about 2 cups)
1 (14-ounce) can Eagle® Brand
Sweetened Condensed Milk
(NOT evaporated milk)
1 cup cold water
⅓ cup ReaLemon® Lemon Juice from
Concentrate
2 cups ice cubes

In blender container, combine all ingredients except ice; blend well. Gradually add ice, blending until smooth. Garnish as desired. Refrigerate leftovers. (Mixture stays thick and creamy in refrigerator.)

Strawberry: Omit bananas. Add 1 pint fresh strawberries, cleaned and hulled, *or* 2 cups frozen unsweetened strawberries, partially thawed, and few drops red food coloring if desired. Proceed as above.

Strawberry-Banana: Reduce bananas to ½ cup; add 1½ cups fresh strawberries *or* 1 cup frozen unsweetened strawberries, partially thawed. Proceed as above.

Orange-Banana: Omit 1 banana and reduce ReaLemon® brand to ¼ cup. Use 1 cup orange juice instead of water. Proceed as above.

Pineapple: Omit bananas. Add 1 (8-ounce) can juice-pack crushed pineapple. Proceed as above.

MIXER METHOD: Omit ice cubes. In large mixer bowl, mash fruit; gradually beat in ReaLemon® brand, sweetened condensed milk and 2½ cups cold water. Chill before serving.

STRAWBERRY SHAKE (TOP),
BANANA SHAKE (BOTTOM)

HOMEMADE CREAM LIQUEURS—MINT, ORANGE, COFFEE

HOMEMADE CREAM LIQUEURS

Makes about 1 quart

1 (14-ounce) can Eagle® Brand Sweetened Condensed Milk (NOT evaporated milk)
1¼ cups flavored liqueur (almond, coffee, orange *or* mint)
2 cups (1 pint) Borden® Whipping Cream *or* Coffee Cream

In blender container, combine ingredients; blend until smooth. Serve over ice. Garnish as desired. Store tightly covered in refrigerator. Stir before serving.

CREAMY HOT CHOCOLATE BASE

Makes about 2½ cups

1 (14-ounce) can Eagle® Brand Sweetened Condensed Milk (NOT evaporated milk)
4 (1-ounce) squares semi-sweet chocolate
1 cup (½ pint) Borden® Coffee Cream
Hot milk or water

In medium saucepan, over low heat, combine sweetened condensed milk and chocolate; cook and stir until chocolate melts. Remove from heat; cool to room temperature. Add cream; mix well. Store tightly covered in refrigerator. For each serving, combine ¼ *cup* chocolate base and ½ *cup* hot milk; mix well. Serve immediately.

HOMEMADE IRISH CREAM LIQUEUR

Makes about 5 cups

1¼ to 1¾ cups Irish whiskey, brandy, rum, bourbon, scotch *or* rye whiskey
1 (14-ounce) can Eagle® Brand Sweetened Condensed Milk (NOT evaporated milk)
2 cups (1 pint) Borden® Whipping Cream *or* Coffee Cream
2 tablespoons chocolate-flavored syrup
2 teaspoons instant coffee
1 teaspoon vanilla extract
½ teaspoon almond extract

In blender container, combine ingredients; blend until smooth. Serve over ice. Garnish as desired. Store tightly covered in refrigerator. Stir before serving.

CHERRY CREAM PUNCH

Makes about 3½ quarts

2 (14-ounce) cans Eagle® Brand Sweetened Condensed Milk (NOT evaporated milk)
1 to 1½ cups kirsch or other cherry-flavored liqueur
¼ cup grenadine syrup
2 (32-ounce) bottles club soda, chilled
Borden® Cherry Vanilla Ice Cream

In large punch bowl, combine sweetened condensed milk, kirsch and grenadine. Just before serving, add club soda and scoops of ice cream. Refrigerate leftovers.

STRAWBERRY-BANANA PUNCH

Makes about 2½ quarts

3 ripe bananas, cut up (about 2 cups)
1 pint fresh strawberries, cleaned and hulled
1 (14-ounce) can Eagle® Brand Sweetened Condensed Milk (NOT evaporated milk)
¼ cup ReaLemon® Lemon Juice from Concentrate
2 (32-ounce) bottles ginger ale, chilled

In blender container, combine all ingredients except ginger ale; blend until smooth. Pour into punch bowl. Just before serving, gradually add ginger ale. Serve over ice. Refrigerate leftovers.

CREAMY HOT CHOCOLATE

Makes about 2 quarts

1 (14-ounce) can Eagle® Brand Sweetened Condensed Milk (NOT evaporated milk)
½ cup unsweetened cocoa
1½ teaspoons vanilla extract
⅛ teaspoon salt
6½ cups hot water
Campfire® Marshmallows, optional

In large saucepan, combine sweetened condensed milk, cocoa, vanilla and salt; mix well. Over medium heat, slowly stir in water; heat through, stirring occasionally. Top with marshmallows if desired. Refrigerate leftovers.

MICROWAVE: In 2-quart glass measure, combine all ingredients except marshmallows. Heat on 100% power (high) 8 to 10 minutes, stirring every 3 minutes. Top with marshmallows if desired.

Tip: Chocolate can be stored in refrigerator up to 5 days. Mix well and reheat before serving.

CREAMY HOT CHOCOLATE

BRANDY MILK PUNCH

Makes about 3 quarts

5 cups Borden® Milk
2 (14-ounce) cans Eagle® Brand Sweetened Condensed Milk (NOT evaporated milk)
1 to 1½ cups brandy
1 cup light rum
1 cup (½ pint) Borden® Whipping Cream, whipped
Ground nutmeg

In large punch bowl, combine milk and sweetened condensed milk; add brandy and rum. Chill. Fold in whipped cream. Garnish with nutmeg. Refrigerate leftovers.

GRASSHOPPER PUNCH

Makes about 2½ quarts

1 (14-ounce) can Eagle® Brand Sweetened Condensed Milk (NOT evaporated milk)
½ cup green creme de menthe
½ cup white creme de cacao
2 (32-ounce) bottles club soda, chilled Borden® Mint Chocolate Chip Ice Cream

In punch bowl, combine sweetened condensed milk, creme de menthe and creme de cacao; mix well. Just before serving, add club soda and scoops of ice cream. Refrigerate leftovers.

APPLE CINNAMON CREAM LIQUEUR (LEFT),
TROPICAL CREAM PUNCH (RIGHT)

APPLE CINNAMON CREAM LIQUEUR

Makes about 1 quart

1 (14-ounce) can Eagle® Brand
  Sweetened Condensed Milk
  (NOT evaporated milk)
1 cup apple schnapps
2 cups (1 pint) Borden® Whipping
  Cream *or* Half-and-Half
½ teaspoon ground cinnamon

In blender container, combine
ingredients; blend until smooth. Serve
over ice. Garnish as desired. Store
tightly covered in refrigerator. Stir
before serving.

Fuzzy Navel Cream Liqueur: Omit
apple schnapps and cinnamon. Add 1
cup peach schnapps and ¼ cup frozen
orange juice concentrate, thawed.
Proceed as above.

TROPICAL CREAM PUNCH

Makes about 3 quarts

1 (14-ounce) can Eagle® Brand
  Sweetened Condensed Milk
  (NOT evaporated milk)
1 (6-ounce) can frozen orange juice
  concentrate, thawed
1 (6-ounce) can frozen pineapple juice
  concentrate, thawed
2 (32-ounce) bottles club soda, chilled
  Orange slices

In punch bowl, combine sweetened
condensed milk and juice concentrates;
mix well. Add club soda; stir. Garnish
with orange slices. Serve over ice.
Refrigerate leftovers.

Dessert Making Hints

INTRODUCTION

Eagle Brand is an all-natural concentrated blend of whole milk and sugar condensed by a special vacuum cooking process. It is entirely different from evaporated milk. Eagle Brand may become thicker and more caramel-colored as its age or storage temperature increases. The performance of the product is not affected by these natural changes. The grocer's shelf life indicated on the can is 15 months. However, the unopened product is safe and wholesome indefinitely as long as the can seal is intact. If the sweetened condensed milk becomes unusually thick, stir briskly before using. If the product has become very caramelized, use in recipes where the caramel flavor is compatible with other ingredients. The best storage for sweetened condensed milk is a cool, dry place.

Because it is a natural product, Eagle Brand may vary in color and consistency from can to can. These two photos illustrate the normal differences which may occur in Eagle Brand over time.

HINTS FOR USING EAGLE BRAND

- Remove entire end of can with can opener; then use rubber scraper to remove all of the sweetened condensed milk from the can.

- To avoid lumps in a cream cheese base recipe, gradually beat sweetened condensed milk into beaten cream cheese.

- Always heat sweetened condensed milk and chocolate over low or medium heat, stirring constantly.

- To avoid lumpy gelatine mixtures, sprinkle unflavored gelatine over cold water; let stand 1 minute. Cook and stir over *low* heat until dissolved.

- Always store any unused sweetened condensed milk in refrigerator in covered container. Use within a week.

EAGLE BRAND IS PRESWEETENED

Because Eagle Brand contains sugar which has already been thoroughly dissolved in the manufacturing process, most Eagle Brand recipes require no additional sugar.

EAGLE BRAND & CHOCOLATE

When heated with chocolate, Eagle Brand quickly thickens to a velvety smooth consistency for candies and sauces that are never grainy or long-cooking. There's no need for constant stirring or a candy thermometer.

MAGIC THICKENING

Because it is a precooked blend of milk and sugar, Eagle Brand thickens almost magically with the addition of acidic fruit juices—to form delicious pie fillings, puddings and desserts *without cooking*. Lemon juice or orange juice concentrate works best.

ICE CREAM MAKING

The thick creamy consistency of Eagle Brand helps to minimize the formation of large ice crystals in ice creams and frozen desserts.

A NOTE ABOUT EGGS

Some recipes in this book specify, "Use only Grade A clean, uncracked eggs." This is a precaution given when uncooked eggs are called for—egg nog, meringues or pie fillings, etc.

HOW TO CARAMELIZE EAGLE® BRAND SWEETENED CONDENSED MILK

OVEN METHOD: Preheat oven to 425°. Pour 1 can sweetened condensed milk into 8- or 9-inch pie plate. Cover with aluminum foil; place in shallow pan. Fill pan with hot water. Bake 1 to 1½ hours or until thick and light caramel-colored. Remove foil; cool. Chill.

STOVETOP METHOD: Pour 1 can sweetened condensed milk into top of double boiler; cover. Place over boiling water. Over low heat, simmer 1 to 1½ hours or until thick and light caramel-colored. Beat until smooth. Cool. Chill.

MICROWAVE METHOD: Pour 1 can sweetened condensed milk into 2-quart glass measure. Cook on 50% power (medium) 4 minutes, stirring after 2 minutes. Reduce to 30% power (medium-low); cook 12 to 18 minutes or until thick and light caramel-colored, stirring briskly every 2 minutes until smooth. Cool. Chill.

TO REHEAT: Place desired amount of caramel in a 1- or 2-cup glass measure. Heat on 100% power (high) 40 to 50 seconds or until warm, stirring after 20 seconds.

CAUTION: NEVER HEAT UNOPENED CAN.

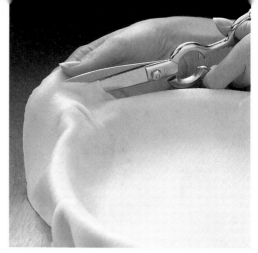

CRUMB CRUST

Makes one 8- or 9-inch crust

1½ cups graham cracker or chocolate wafer crumbs

¼ cup sugar

6 tablespoons margarine or butter, melted

Combine ingredients; mix well. Press firmly on bottom and up side to rim of 8- or 9-inch pie plate. Chill thoroughly or bake in preheated 375° oven 6 to 8 minutes or until edges are brown. Cool before filling.

Use kitchen shears or sharp knife to trim dough ½ inch beyond pie plate edge. Fold under extra dough to form rim.

PASTRY CRUST

Makes one 8- or 9-inch crust

1 cup unsifted flour

½ teaspoon salt

⅓ cup shortening

3 to 4 tablespoons cold water

In medium bowl, combine flour and salt; cut in shortening until mixture resembles coarse corn meal. Sprinkle with water, 1 tablespoon at a time, mixing until dough is just moist enough to hold together. Form dough into ball. Place on well-floured surface. Press down into a flat circle with smooth edges. Roll dough to a circle ⅛-inch thick and about 1½ inches larger than inverted pie plate. Ease dough into pie plate. Trim ½ inch beyond pie plate edge. Fold under; flute edge as desired.

Flute edge as desired.

TO BAKE WITHOUT FILLING

Preheat oven to 450°. Prick bottom and side of pastry shell with fork. Line pastry with aluminum foil; fill with dry beans. Bake 5 minutes; remove beans and foil. Bake 5 to 7 minutes longer or until golden.

TO BAKE WITH FILLING

Preheat oven as directed in recipe. Do not prick pastry shell. Fill and bake as directed.

To keep an unfilled pastry crust from puffing or shrinking during baking, line with aluminum foil and fill with dry beans.

FOR SUCCESSFUL MERINGUE

- Weather affects meringues. When the humidity is high, the sugar in the meringue absorbs moisture from the air, making the meringue gooey and limp. Meringues should be made on sunny, dry days.

- Carefully separate egg whites from the yolks (they separate best when cold).

- Mixing bowls and beaters should be completely grease-free.

- Egg whites should come to room temperature before beating. This increases the volume.

- Sugar should be added *gradually*. Continue beating until sugar is completely dissolved.

For Successful Meringue

- Cool meringue slowly, away from drafts to prevent shrinking and weeping.

MERINGUE

For 8- or 9-inch pie

3 egg whites
¼ teaspoon cream of tartar
6 tablespoons sugar

Preheat oven to 350°. In small mixer bowl, beat egg whites with cream of tartar until soft peaks form; gradually add sugar, beating until stiff but not dry. Spread meringue on top of pie, sealing carefully to edge of pastry shell. Bake 12 to 15 minutes or until golden brown. Cool. Chill thoroughly.

1. Beat egg whites and cream of tartar to *soft peaks* before adding sugar.

2. *Gradually* add sugar, beating until *stiff* but not dry. Mixture should be glossy.

3. Spread meringue, sealing carefully to edge of pastry shell.

4. Brown meringue as directed. Cool *slowly*.

TINTING COCONUT

Dilute few drops food coloring with ½ teaspoon water or milk. Add coconut; toss with fork until evenly tinted.

TOASTING COCONUT AND NUTS

Spread coconut or nuts evenly in shallow pan. Toast in preheated 350° oven 7 to 15 minutes or until golden, stirring frequently.

FROSTING GRAPES

Dip small clusters of grapes into slightly beaten egg white; sprinkle with granulated sugar. Dry on wire racks.

CHOCOLATE LEAVES

Coat undersides of real leaves lightly with vegetable oil. Melt semi-sweet chocolate and coat undersides of leaves thickly with chocolate using small spoon. Chill or freeze until firm, then peel away leaf.

CHOCOLATE CURLS

With a vegetable parer or thin, sharp knife, slice across block of sweet milk chocolate or large-size milk chocolate candy bar with long, thin strokes. Chocolate should be at room temperature.

PASTRY EGG WASH

For a more golden crust on a 2-crust pie, beat 1 egg yolk with 2 tablespoons water; brush evenly over pastry before baking.

To split cake layer, measure halfway up side; mark with toothpicks. Using long piece of thread, rest on picks. Cross thread and pull through to split layers.

For level layers, use a long thin serrated knife to slice off rounded or uneven top of cake.

MAKE-AHEAD WHIPPED CREAM

Freeze dollops of whipped cream on waxed paper-lined baking sheets. When frozen, store in tightly closed plastic bags for use on desserts or Irish coffee.

FOR BAKED ALASKAS

Ice cream must be very firm before it is covered with meringue and baked. Dessert can be frozen several days before serving.

UNMOLDING FROZEN DESSERTS

For easy unmolding of ice cream desserts, line container with aluminum foil, extending foil beyond rim of container. When frozen, lift dessert from pan with foil.

SLICING HINTS

- Use a wet knife for cutting desserts with meringue. Wipe off knife after each cut.

- Use a damp knife with a thin blade for slicing cake rolls.

- Use a damp knife with a firm blade for cutting fudge or candy.

- Use a serrated knife for slicing angel food cakes.

WHIPPING CREAM

- Chill beaters and bowl thoroughly.

- Beat chilled whipping cream on high speed (overbeating or beating on low speed can cause cream to separate into fat and liquid).

- Beat only until stiff. Whipping cream doubles in volume.

- To sweeten whipped cream, gradually beat in 1 to 2 tablespoons granulated or confectioners' sugar and ½ to 1 teaspoon vanilla extract for each cup unwhipped whipping cream.

To marble, gently swirl a narrow spatula through the light and dark mixtures.

Beat whipping cream only until *stiff* peaks form.

Index